# Zen Action

THE UNIVERSITY PRESS OF HAWAII / *Honolulu*

# Zen Person

*by* T. P. Kasulis

Permission to reprint passages from the following
sources is gratefully acknowledged.

*Zen Comments on the Mumonkan* by Zenkei Shibayama,
© 1974 by Zenkei Shibayama. Reprinted by permission
of Harper & Row Publishers Inc.

*The Zen Master Hakuin: Selected Writings*, tr. Philip
Yampolsky, © 1971 by Columbia University Press.
Reprinted by permission of Columbia University Press.

**Library of Congress Cataloging in Publication Data**

Kasulis, T P    1948–
    Zen action/zen person.

    Bibliography: p.
    Includes index.
        1.  Zen Buddhism—Doctrines.   2.   Philosophy, Buddhist.
I.   Title.
BQ9268.6.K37        294.3'4        80–27858
ISBN 0–8248–0702–2

To my father

# Contents

# Preface

"You have asked permission to practice Zen meditation in this temple, but tell me: What is Zen?"

After some hesitation and embarrassed smiling, I said something about Zen's being a way of life rather than a set of dogmas.

Laughter filled the tatami-matted reception room. "Everyone comes here to study Zen, but none of them knows what Zen is. Zen is . . . knowing thyself. You are a Western philosopher and you know of Socrates' quest. Did you assume Zen would be something different?"

At least from the time of Socrates, Western thinkers have been concerned with human nature. What am I? What is my relationship with the people and things around me? What ought I to do? In the twentieth century, we in the Western world generally believe that there is no substance or essence constituting our humanness; our identity as persons is developed, not given. As communication among the peoples of the world increases, it is natural for us to wonder how those in other places address these same concerns. This book is a study of what it means to become a person in Japanese Zen Buddhism. Since the approach is philosophical, however, it is above all an inquiry into ourselves.

That Zen Buddhism resists philosophical explication is a thesis more Western than Japanese. Thus, many Japanese scholars recognize Dōgen, a thirteenth-century Zen Master, as their country's most profound thinker. With his piercing analytic skills and comprehensive knowledge of the Chinese philosophical classics, Dōgen brought philosophy and Zen Buddhism closer together than they had ever been before. In fact he played a role not unlike that of a

Western theologian, especially one of a phenomenological or existential bent. The Zen influence on modern Japanese thought is
also unmistakable. The most respected systematic philosopher of
modern Japan, NISHIDA Kitarō,* was a devout Zen Buddhist who
utilized Western terminology to develop a philosophical system that
would account for the distinctively Zen Buddhist religious experience. Two other prominent thinkers of the modern Kyoto school,
WATSUJI Tetsurō and TANABE Hajime, wrote monographs on
Dōgen's philosophical significance.

This does not imply, of course, that Zen Buddhism is *primarily* a
philosophy; it certainly qualifies more as a spiritual or religious
way of life. Studying about Zen should never be confused with
practicing Zen, just as studying aesthetics should not be confused
with being an artist. The point is that Zen Buddhism, like other
religions, incorporates at least an implicit philosophical standpoint
—a standpoint that can be described and analyzed in its own
terms. Bearing this distinction in mind, we can avoid much of
the confusion surrounding the relationship between Zen and
philosophy.

Accepting the possibility of a philosophical study of Zen Buddhism, we must ask how such a study should be structured. The
focus in this book is on the Zen Buddhist view of the *person*. There
are three specific reasons for choosing this theme. First, what is
most distinctive in Zen Buddhism and potentially of most interest
to Western philosophy is its phenomenology of prereflective
experience—especially insofar as that phenomenology addresses
itself to the basis of thinking, the epistemology of self-consciousness,
the meaning of personal freedom, and the interrelationships among
spiritual, aesthetic, and moral sensitivities. Since all of these
elements can be seen as aspects of the *personal* realm, this one
focus will concentrate our attention on what is of most philosophical relevance.

The second reason for concentrating on the person is method-

*This study gives East Asian names in the traditional order—surnames first—unless
the individual has established a preference for the Western order (for example,
D. T. SUZUKI or Wing-tsit CHAN). To prevent confusion, when a person's full name is
given, the surname will appear in uppercase letters.

ological. In a philosophical study of Zen Buddhism, an obvious starting point is the interpretations offered by historical and modern Zen Masters. Although these writings do reveal the crucial concepts of the Zen tradition, often the explanations are not fully satisfying to the critical Western reader. To fill in the gaps, we will resort in this study to some philosophical reconstruction. In other words, by extrapolating from the basic tenets of the Zen tradition, we can reason through certain arguments that are only implicit or fragmented in the Zen writings themselves. This is, of course, a hazardous enterprise, and we need some method of ensuring that our reconstructions are not merely the products of runaway specu-lation. As we have noted, Zen Buddhism is not primarily a philo-sophical theory about the meaning of the person; rather, it is a religious tradition designed to help people in various ways. Throughout this book, we will be checking our reconstructions of the Zen view of the person by seeing whether they are in accord with actual Zen *practice*. Our interpretation will ultimately be based not only on what Zen Masters say, but also on how they act —particularly in relations with their disciples. To whatever extent Zen advocates an ideal of the person along with its general descrip-tion of human nature, that ideal should be apparent in what the disciples are being trained to become.

The third reason for our attention on the person is that this topic will show us to what degree Japanese Zen Buddhism is the product of a particular culture. While an idea of truth or reality, for exam-ple, may claim to be universal in application, the concept of the person is tied to cultural heritage. No comprehensive philosophy, certainly no religion, can be completely independent of its cultural context, nor should it try to be. Even though the significance of our investigation may ultimately transcend culture, a preliminary understanding of the cultural setting will clarify why certain inter-pretations are presented in the way they are. The study of the Japanese cultural milieu is by no means a major aspect of this book, but a few rudimentary points should prove helpful. In in-troducing this topic, we are already looking ahead to the first chapter.

# Acknowledgments

I wish to express my gratitude to the following people and organizations for their assistance.

My colleagues in the University of Hawaii's Department of Philosophy, who read the manuscript in various stages and supplied valuable criticism and moral support.

Professors Robert S. Brumbaugh, Edward S. Casey, and John E. Smith, who supervised the parts of this work first appearing as my dissertation at Yale.

Professors Hajime Nakamura, Director of the Eastern Institute in Tokyo, and Paul Wienpahl, Professor of Philosophy at UC/Santa Barbara, who took the time to read an earlier version of the text and discuss aspects of it with me in detail.

The editors of the *Journal of Chinese Philosophy* and the *International Philosophical Quarterly* for permission to incorporate material that in earlier versions appeared as the following articles: "The Absolute and the Relative in Taoist Philosophy," *JCP* 4 (1977); "The Two Strands of Nothingness," *IPQ* 19 (March 1979).

The American Council of Learned Societies and the University of Hawaii Research and Training Revolving Fund, sources of financial support and encouragement in my research.

My students at the University of Hawaii, especially Shigenori Nagatomo, David Shaner, and Richard Swingle, whose perceptive questions sustained my interest in the issues raised in this work.

Floris Sakamoto, Richard Swingle, and Stuart Kiang, who offered invaluable assistance in preparing and editing the final manuscript.

Bishop Kyodo Fujihana of the Jodo Mission of Hawaii, who generously contributed the calligraphy reproduced on the cover of this book.

Ellen, Telemachus, and Matthias Kasulis, who tolerated patiently my needs for solitude in the larger environment of love and sharing.

Errors in this work, if any, are my own.

# Part I
## THE CONTEXT OF NOTHINGNESS

# CHAPTER 1

# The Cultural Setting: Context and Personal Meaning

To grasp the meaning of the person in Japanese Zen Buddhism, we must recognize that this form of Buddhist thought developed within a specific culture. Although in any society there is a significant divergence between the way a person is viewed religiously and secularly, religion always finds itself in interplay with the secular and can never be fully independent of it. A discussion of how the person is generally viewed in Japan is, therefore, a logical starting point for the specific project of investigating the meaning of the person in Japanese Zen Buddhism. In cultures as diverse as those of Japan and America, we must be wary of unconsciously projecting inappropriate categories onto the Japanese experience. To restrict this discussion, we will draw examples from what is shared most explicitly by the secular and religious dimensions of Japanese culture: language. Specifically, we will make some observations about the possibilities for expressing the personal sphere within the Japanese language itself.

## THREE JAPANESE WORDS FOR "PERSON"

Although in Japanese, as in English, several terms may be used to designate the person, three common words are especially illuminating for our purposes. Juxtaposing them will help clarify how Japanese generally view the relationship between context and individual. The three words are *hito* ("man"), *kojin* ("individual"), and *ningen* ("human being").

Before analyzing these terms in detail, a few preliminary remarks about the nature and development of the Japanese language are in order. Because of the way writing was introduced into Japan, the Japanese commonly distinguish native Japanese words *(wago no kotoba)* from words borrowed from China *(kango no kotoba)*. Originally, many Japanese words were assigned (usually single) Chinese characters having the same meaning; such words continued to be pronounced as they had been in Japanese. Since the Chinese culture was older and more fully developed at the time, however, the Japanese also found it useful to borrow many Chinese words lacking Japanese equivalents, attempting to pronounce them like the Chinese. The resultant situation is not much different from that in English, where words have Anglo-Saxon and Graeco-Roman origins. That is, the words needed for everyday use tend to come from the indigenous language and the more abstract, technical terms from the lending language. In English, for instance, *thinking* (the Anglo-Saxon word) serves well for ordinary purposes, but more precise considerations might lead us to distinguish *cogitation, ratiocination, meditation, reflection,* and so forth (all Graeco-Roman words).

In Japanese, the relationship between *wago* and *kango* is similar, but the Japanese have to be more aware of the difference than do their English-speaking counterparts. First, the same character is pronounced differently in *wago* and *kango* (the *kun* and *on* readings). Therefore, the same character may be pronounced *hito, NIN,* or *JIN.* (By convention, the uppercase letters indicate the *on* pronunciation of *kango.*) Second, because of the way dictionaries are arranged, a Japanese will find it convenient (and often necessary) to consult different dictionaries for words derived from *wago* and *kango.* An English speaker might appreciate the practical impact of this distinction if, say, English used a totally different pronunciation for consonants, depending on whether the word were of Anglo-Saxon or Graeco-Roman origin. This is roughly the situation for the Japanese, and it is obvious why they tend to make such a clear distinction between the two "languages" constituting Japanese. They consider *wago* to be more concrete, emotive, and traditionally Japanese than *kango.* With these linguistic factors in mind, we can now turn to our analysis of the three terms.

1.  *Hito* (人)—"man, person, people, character" as in:
    *(a)* "Who is that *person* over there?" *
    *(b)* "What kind of *man* (person) is he?"
2.  *Kojin* (個人)—"an individual, a private person (*KO* = "an individual" or a counter for enumerating; *JIN* = "man") as in:
    *(c)* "*private* (personal) feelings"
    *(d)* "As an *individual*, what do you think?"
    *(e)* "He is *personally* a nice fellow."
    *(f)* "individualism"
3.  *Ningen* (人間)—"human being, person, man" (*NIN* = "man"; *GEN* = "interval, relationship, betweenness") as in:
    *(g)* "Treat them more like *human beings*."
    *(h)* "*human* society"
    *(i)* "A *man's* worth lies not so much in what he has as in what he is."

*Hito*, one of the most common words in Japanese, is used in a variety of senses to indicate a person, people (in general, there is no singular/plural distinction in Japanese), and sometimes, by extension, even humankind. Etymologically, it is a native Japanese word *(wago no kotoba)*, written with a single character and retaining its relatively concrete, phenomenalistic connotation—that is, the *hito* is the person one perceives in everyday affairs. Befitting its significance, the character itself is a pictograph: a simplified drawing of a stick figure's body and legs. But this same character can also be used in combination with other characters to form more complex words. In such cases it usually assumes the *on* pronunciation of *JIN*

*Examples are based on standard usages of the terms as cited in Koh MASUDA, ed.. *Kenkyusha's New Japanese-English Dictionary*:

*(a)* あの人は誰ですか。
*(b)* どんな人ですか。
*(c)* 個人の感情
*(d)* 一個人としてどう思うか。
*(e)* 彼は個人としては好い人だ。
*(f)* 個人主義
*(g)* もっと人間らしく待遇せよ。
*(h)* 人間社会
*(i)* 人間の価値は財産にあらずしてその人物にある。

or *NIN*. This change is found, for example, in the Japanese word for individual: *kojin*.

As we see in the preceding list, when the Japanese single out an "individual," they add the character *KO* to the basic *JIN (hito)*. Significantly, the former character also functions as a suffix in enumerating countable objects. Thus, to see someone as an "individual" *(kojin)* is to see that person as one object among many, an individual extracted from the context of the group for purposes of enumeration. This description clearly lacks the force of the term *individual* conveyed in Western languages. (Consider, for example, Kierkegaard's epitaph: "That Individual.") The English word *individual* (in the sense of a single human being) has strongly per- sonalistic nuances; the Japanese equivalent, *kojin*, is more physicalistic or logical. Consequently, a Western discussion of the person might well start with the individual, but a Japanese discus- sion would probably not begin with the *kojin*.[1] What if we proceed in the other direction, then, adding a character for context *(aida, ma, GEN)* to the basic word *hito*? This gives us the word *ningen*.

*Ningen* is also a popular equivalent for "human being" or "man"; in many situations, its meaning is close to that of *hito*. Perhaps because it is a two-character word (with an *on* or "Chinese" reading), however, it has a somewhat more intellectual connotation than *hito*; it tends to be used in talking about humani- ty generically, for example, rather than about the physical human being. What is more significant, though, is the comparison between *ningen* and *kojin*. Following our analysis of the constituent characters, when the Japanese see someone as an "individual" *(kojin)*, they see him or her as one object among many, but when they see someone as a "human being" *(ningen)*, they see that person in a context. From the Japanese point of view, the person is not primarily an individual subsequently placed within the world. Rather, as indicated by the very structure of the word for "human being," the person is *always* in a context, in a necessary relation- ship with what is around him or her.

This emphasis on the contextual significance of the person is by no means limited linguistically to the meaning of individual terms, however. It pervades the pragmatic and syntactic usage of the lan- guage in interpersonal relationships as well.

## CONTEXTUAL MEANING IN INTERPERSONAL COMMUNICATION

There is an important distinction to be made between the way Westerners and Japanese see the function of language. Suppose we represent interpersonal communication as $aRb$, where $a$ and $b$ are persons and $R$ is the linguistic medium through which they communicate. The Western view typically regards $a$ and $b$ as two transmitters, each emitting signals to be received and interpreted by the other. In English, for example, we speak of language as a bridge spanning the gap between $I$ and $you$. The isolated $a$ and $b$ together create an $R$ so that communication can take place. In Japan, however, the event is viewed quite differently: the $R$ is primary. The $R$ is the given out of which $a$ and $b$ take their shape. Accordingly, although the Japanese language does not lack personal pronouns, it is generally considered improper or even impolite to use them except when absolutely necessary for comprehension. In this regard, they are often used almost like proper nouns rather than pronouns in our sense. Thus the conscious bifurcation between $I$ and $you$ is diminished. In fact, when reference to the personal is unavoidable, the Japanese often use directional words rather than personal pronouns. Suppose, for example, two people bump into each other on the street:

| English | Japanese | Literal translation |
|---------|----------|---------------------|
| "Oh, excuse me." | "Sumimasen." | "[Indebtedness] does not end." |
| "Oh no, excuse me." | "Iie, kochirakoso." | "Oh no. This way [goes the indebtedness]." |

In the Japanese version, the emphasis is on the relationship (the indebtedness) and its direction, not on the people who created the situation. That they talk about the direction of the indebtedness without naming it exemplifies to what extent the relationship is assumed. If there were no such relation, the two people would not even be speaking to each other. Another way of avoiding direct reference to individuals is through the use of the word kata as a polite equivalent for "person" (hito). The character kata fundamentally means "direction," so that instead of saying "this person" *(kono hito)*, the Japanese consider it more polite to say "this direction" *(kono kata)*. Thus, we again note that the Japanese often refer to the person by pointing to an orientation—that is, by indicating *which side* of the relationship is being considered. In fact, the ordinary word for "you" is *anata*, a classical word meaning "in that direction." This usage only makes sense if language is being spoken from the perspective of the R and not *a* or *b*. The *a* and *b*—the *I* and *you*—only become meaningful insofar as the R, the context of the language used in a given instance, *gives* them meaning.

The Japanese language emphasizes the context of interpersonal communication in yet another way—namely, by referring to the comparative status of speaker and listener. With its honorific/humble and polite/informal forms, Japanese requires each conversant to understand his or her position vis-à-vis the other person. In most social situations, a conversation between strangers can hardly begin until there has been an exchange of business cards or an introduction by an intermediary so that each party is aware of the other person's relative status. In other words, a *context* must exist before the two people can begin to relate formally to each other. This context might be permanent and objective (father/son or employer/employee) or temporary and subjective (for example, a business relationship determined by who is doing a favor for whom and the degree to which the favor is expected or extraordinary), but in either case it defines the way in which the two persons will interrelate. Again, in terms of the original model, *a* and *b* assume meaning only in reference to the R. Without a clearly established context, people are individually distinguishable, but meaningless as persons in the full sense.

This brief investigation of Japanese linguistic and communicative modes leads to the conclusion that in Japan the context is given primacy over the individual: the context defines and elaborates the individual rather than vice versa. This conclusion is not at all original, of course, and we might have arrived at the same point by analyzing other aspects of the culture. NAKAMURA Hajime, for example, argues convincingly along the same lines in his analysis of the Japanese sense of proprieties:

Due to the stress on social proprieties in Japan another characteristic of its culture appears—the tendency of social relationships to supersede or take precedence over the individual. . . . When this type of thinking is predominant, consciousness of the individual as an entity appears always in the wider sphere of consciousness of social relationships, although the significance of the individual is still recognized.[2]

Thus, Nakamura's analysis agrees with our observation that while the "individual" *(kojin)* is a real entity, one most fully becomes a "human being" *(ningen)* when one is in relationship to one's surroundings.

Whatever ultimate meaning a Japanese may achieve, it is clear that that meaning is viewed from a perspective different from the one customarily taken in the West. The notion that the world is a stage and we are the actors is not Japanese. For the Japanese the world, the human context, is not a static backdrop against which people play out their individual roles. Rather the context is an organic reality, transforming itself to the rhythm of its own necessity, establishing the interrelationships that define individual persons. In Japan, personal significance always occurs *in medias res;* it arises out of the demands of the social, linguistic, or philosophical framework. The individual becomes meaningful insofar as he or she is an outgrowth of the relationships established by the operative context, not vice versa. Taking note of this special use of the term *context* and its relevance to the Japanese understanding of the person, let us now focus our attention more specifically on Zen Buddhism.

## THE ZEN CONTEXT OF THE PERSON

If Japanese Zen Buddhism is characteristically Japanese, we might expect to find in it a special context that serves as the ground of both the universality and the individuality of the person: universality in that one's meaning as a person is derived from a context beyond the bounds of one's egocentrism; individuality in that one is defined as a person by one's unique set of interrelationships. This context should also be distinctively Buddhist insofar as it serves as the specific framework of Japanese Zen Buddhism, though not of

Japanese culture at large. Zen does, in fact, establish such a context, one traditionally characterized by the bewildering name of *mu:* nothingness. Let us begin our inquiry with one of the most famous Zen koans:

> A *monk once asked Master Joshu [Ch: Chao-chou],* * "Has a dog the Buddha Nature or not?" Joshu said, "Mu!"*[3]

To appreciate Jōshū's response, we must investigate the thrust of the question. It is standard Zen Buddhist doctrine that every sentient being has Buddha-nature.† Since any Zen monk would know this, we must assume that the point of the inquiry was something other than the literal question. The exchange constitutes a koan, a Zen Master's paradoxical utterance later used as a meditative focus for Zen training. The dynamics of koan practice will be studied in a later chapter. For now, we need only note that the monk is challenging Jōshū by posing a question with no apparent solution: if Jōshū responds in the affirmative, he is open to censure for being overly dependent on traditional teachings instead of his own insight; if he responds negatively, he can be criticized for egotism and arrogance, for placing himself above the teachings of his Buddhist predecessors.[4] Furthermore, he is to answer the question immediately, without deliberation or hesitation. In this situation, Jōshū responds *"Mu!"* In his thirteenth-century commentary, the Chinese master Mumon (Ch: Wu-mên Hui-k'ai) advises us not to take this *mu* in its literal sense of no:

> The dog! The Buddha Nature!
> The truth is manifested in full.
> A moment of yes-and-no:[5]
> Lost are your body and soul.[6]

---

*Since Chinese Zen Masters and scriptures are usually known to Japanese Zen Buddhists only by the Japanized pronunciation of their names, this book will use that form. For reference, however, the proper Chinese pronunciation of each name is given in parentheses at its first appearance.
†Buddha-nature—the intrinsic natural quality by which any (usually sentient) being can attain enlightenment or because of which we can say all beings are already perfect or enlightened (at least potentially). As we will see later in our discussion of Dōgen, this understanding of Buddha-nature is sometimes challenged.

The Zen position is that all intellectual attempts to grasp the significance of this utterance will fail. Mumon continues:

> In studying Zen, one must pass the barriers set up by ancient Zen Masters. . . . Now, tell me, what is the barrier of the Zen Masters? Just this "Mu"—it is the barrier of Zen. . . . Don't you want to pass the barrier? Then concentrate yourself into this "Mu," with your 360 bones and 84,000 pores, making your whole body into one great inquiry. Day and night work intently at it. Do not attempt nihilistic or dualistic interpretations. . . .
> Now, how should one strive? With might and main work at this "Mu," and be "Mu." If you do not stop or waver in your striving, then behold, when the dharma candle is lighted, darkness is at once enlightened.[7]

The warning about "nihilistic or dualistic interpretations" is more than mere rhetoric. We must resist the temptation to think of *mu* either as an indeterminate void or as something relative and completely open to conceptual analysis. Mumon exhorts the Zen student to work at *mu*, to *become* it, rather than to understand it. This account may be efficacious for training purposes, but for our philosophical concerns it gives no starting point. If we look to Zen Masters for further explication, we encounter more statements like those of Mumon—admonitions against objectifying *mu*, but no detailed explanation of *why* it must not be objectified. Certainly, from what we have already said about the contextual meaning of the person, this reticence is understandable. If *mu* or nothingness is the context within which Zen persons find their identity, it is clear that Zen Buddhists should not try to stand outside that context in order to understand it. As Mumon advises, one must *be mu*, not think about it. Yet a philosophy of Zen Buddhism must ask why *mu* has this special place in Zen. Why can it not be objectified and analyzed? Fortunately, the Zen Masters at least hint at how we might resolve our difficulty.

## TWO STRANDS OF NOTHINGNESS

Despite stylistic differences, Zen Masters share a common heritage and, to a certain extent, a set of traditional interpretations.

Specifically, in discussions of *mu* we find two recurrent themes. First, words (and the concepts based on them) are ultimately *empty* and to be mistrusted as a medium for fully understanding the nature of experience (or of reality). Second, the Zen student is advised to return to the nondiscriminating *source* of his or her experience (or of reality). Let us see how these two themes apply to the analysis of Jōshū's *mu*.

On one level, Jōshū's response points to the emptiness within the question itself. The Zen student must learn not to think of linguistic distinctions as always referring to ontically distinct realities. According to Buddhist doctrine, the dog has Buddha-nature if it is a sentient being. But what is a sentient being? Can it be conceived independently of nonsentient beings? Experientially, there is only the dog and the concept of Buddha-nature; in his poem, Mumon juxtaposes the two without asserting any relationship between them. In the immediacy of seeing the dog, there is no metaphysical analysis.

In his commentary on the *mu* koan, a present-day Zen Master, YASUTANI Hakuun, makes explicit this Zen mistrust of conceptualization:

> The opinions you hold and your worldly knowledge are your delusions. Included also are philosophical and moral concepts, no matter how lofty, as well as religious beliefs and dogmas, not to mention innocent, commonplace thoughts. In short, all conceivable ideas are embraced within the term "delusions" and as such are a hindrance to the realization of your Essential-nature. So dissolve them with the fireball of Mu.[8]

Another contemporary Zen Master, SHIBAYAMA Zenkei, emphasizes the same point by referring to a religious experience beyond conceptual dualities:

> The experience of the Buddha Nature itself is creatively expressed here by "Mu." Although literally "Mu" means No, in this case it points to the incomparable satori [enlightenment] which transcends both yes and no, to the religious experience of the Truth one can attain when he casts away his discriminating mind. It has nothing to do with the

dualistic interpretation of yes or no, being and nonbeing. It is Truth itself, the Absolute itself.[9]

In these two passages we find explicit reference to the relativity of all conceptualizations—even those which constitute the doctrines of the Buddhist tradition itself. Jōshū eluded the trap in the monk's question by refusing to be caught in the relative viewpoints affirming or denying the presence of the Buddha-nature in the dog. In this respect, his *"Mu!"* is not a *"No!"* addressed to the question asked. Rather, it is a refusal to accept the conceptual distinctions which give the question meaning.

From another perspective, Jōshū's response can be viewed as a pointing to the nondifferentiated *source* of all things. The dog, the monk, Jōshū himself—all are grounded in something more primordial than either Being or Nonbeing. From this perspective, Jōshū's *mu* is not a refusal to use certain categories but an *affirmation* of an ontological or quasi-ontological category. We turn again to Shibayama's commentary:

Joshu, the questioning monk, and the dog are however only incidental to the story, and they do not have any vital significance in themselves. Unless one grasps the koan within himself as he lives here and now, it ceases to be a real koan. We should not read it as an old story; you yourself have to be directly "Mu" and make not only the monk, but Joshu as well, show the white feather. Then the Buddha Nature is "Mu"; Joshu is "Mu." Not only that, you yourself and the whole universe are nothing but "Mu." Further, "Mu" itself falls far short, it is ever the unnamable "it."[10]

Another contemporary Zen Master, SASAKI Jōshū, is even more explicitly ontological in his language. In his discussion of the *mu* koan, he identifies nothingness with *absolute being*. That is, he maintains that nothingness is the basis of everything:

The human being, believing he belongs to the subjective side and standing in the small mind [that is, viewing the world from the unenlightened perspective of subject/object consciousness], observes absolute being as an object. Actually, that absolute being cannot be an object. Shakyamuni [the historical Buddha] said that absolute being has no color, no form, no voice and exists as nothingness or emptiness. Absolute being works as complete, perfect emptiness and embraces subject and object. If you want to see God or Buddha, you must manifest yourself as emptiness.[11]

In thus speaking of nothingness, Sasaki explicitly uses the term *source:*

Zen is the practice of manifesting yourself as emptiness. When you manifest nothingness, only in that moment do you experience the source of God. When you experience God, Buddha or the source of everything, you don't know what you are doing. When you are completely one with your lover, you don't know whether you are doing something good or bad.[12]

For autobiographical reasons, Shibayama also uses the terminology of the *form of no form:*

My teacher also asked me once, "Show me the form of 'Mu!' " When I said, "It has no form whatsoever," he pressed me, saying, "I want to see that form which has no form." How cutting and drastic! Unless one can freely and clearly present the form of "Mu," it turns out to be a meaningless corpse.[13]

In short, Jōshū's single-word answer has a dual significance, functioning at once as a criticism of conceptual distinctions and as a reference to an ineffable, quasi-ontological source of experience. Although the effectiveness of Jōshū's response is such that the two principles cannot be considered separate and unrelated, it is useful for us to distinguish them in order to isolate two philosophical theses:

1.  Linguistic distinctions (and the concepts formulated through them) cannot be the medium of an adequate description of reality.
2.  Experience (or, alternatively, reality) arises out of a source that cannot be described as either Being or Nonbeing, form or no form.

These two premises recur throughout Zen literature, yet no detailed argument is given in their support. Two explanations are commonly offered to account for this omission. First, as a religious path, Zen Buddhism appeals more to the disciples' *direct* experiences than to their reflective analyses of them. Second, lacking the critical and dialectical powers of their Indian and Western colleagues, East Asian thinkers simply do not see the need for an argument. These two explanations are inadequate. The first begs the question: virtually *all* religious traditions emphasize direct experience over cognitive understanding, yet they often give rational support for their beliefs (through theology, for example). Why does Zen Buddhism not do so? The second explanation overlooks the sophistication of the first thesis. Certainly, it is no naive, uncritical standpoint; it involves an advanced reflection on the nature of language and thought. (In effect, it assumes a metalanguage perspective.) It is unlikely that a cultural tradition would hold such an abstract belief for almost two millennia without some attempt at rational clarification or argument.

There is, however, a third, more persuasive, explanation—namely, no justification is offered for the two Zen theses simply because it has already been offered by traditions influential in the very emergence of Zen Buddhism. Specifically, thesis 1 was argued by Nāgārjuna's Mādhyamika Buddhism and thesis 2 by the Chinese Taoism of Lao Tzŭ and Chuang Tzŭ. To comprehend the philosophical basis of the Zen context of nothingness, therefore, we must temporarily unravel these two main strands and study them individually. This is the project of the next two chapters.

# CHAPTER 2

# Nāgārjuna: The Logic of Emptiness

In this chapter we investigate the first of the two strands of the Zen doctrine of nothingness: the mistrust of conceptualization. Most Western readers know of Zen's predilection for paradoxes and seemingly irrational behavior, as well as its general disregard of philosophical speculation, but this aspect of Zen is usually presented without any articulate rationale, leaving readers to think Zen is grounded in unexamined anti-intellectualism. Some commentators, such as D. T. Suzuki, suggest that Zen's mistrust of conceptualization is a cultural characteristic of the Japanese in general. Ironically, though, the historical roots of the Zen position go back to a radically different cultural situation, one in which all principles, even religious ones, were completely open to philosophical analysis. However much this strand of nothingness may have been interwoven into the larger fabric of the personal context of Zen Buddhism, originally it was part of a comprehensive attempt to demonstrate logically the "emptiness" *(śūnyatā)* of philosophical distinctions. The moving force in this enterprise was the Indian founder of Mādhyamika Buddhism: Nāgārjuna (ca. A.D. 150–250). Although a predecessor to the development of Zen Buddhism, he is, nevertheless, traditionally regarded as a patriarch of the Zen tradition.

## NĀGĀRJUNA: A RESPONSE TO ABHIDHARMA ANALYSIS

Buddhism was originally empirical, practical, and commonsensical; metaphysics and analysis were considered unproductive diversions from the primary task of achieving spiritual liberation. To be concerned with speculative questions, the Buddha claimed, is like being concerned with the origin of a poisoned arrow while it is still in one's flesh, contaminating the bloodstream. The first objective is to remove the arrow—questions about origins to be put off until later.

Within a few centuries after the Buddha's death, however, a highly developed form of scholasticism took hold in India. Many Buddhists were becoming more interested in philosophical analysis than in spiritual self-discipline. They divided into sects, each with its own compendium of high teaching known as its *abhidharma*.[1] They implicitly assumed, for example, that it is not enough to know that craving is the cause of suffering; one also must know exactly what is entailed by the word *cause*. Accepting the distinctions made by various non-Buddhist philosophies, one group held that the effect was potentially contained in the cause, causal change being only a transformation in the appearance of a single substance. An opposing group held that nothing at all continued from the cause into the effect, the two being completely distinct. For the Abhidharma Buddhists, then, analyzing the principles behind Buddhist teachings became almost as important as practicing the teachings. In this climate of bickering and sectarian debate, Nāgārjuna developed his Logic of the Middle based on the doctrine of *śūnyatā* or "emptiness."

Nāgārjuna's project was to demonstrate that the problems of abhidharmic analysis are intrinsically irresolvable; that is, the various philosophical sects of Buddhism were founded on distinctions that must be seen as tentative rather than absolute. Nāgārjuna possessed enough philosophical acumen to realize that he could not make such an assertion without cutting the ground from under his own position. That is, he appreciated the logical paradox of absolutely denying the absoluteness of all philosophical standpoints. His solution to this predicament was both simple and insightful. After drawing up a list of the major distinctions assumed by the various philosophical systems of his time, he demonstrated, one by one, that if these distinctions are considered to be absolute, they lead to ineluctable absurdities. Thus, Nāgārjuna examined various key concepts such as causality, karma, and time, trying to prove abhidharmic analyses invalid. Of course, if the distinctions underlying the philosophical debates are ultimately untenable, then the arguments themselves become empty. Nāgārjuna was thereby able to carry out his critique without taking a position of his own. By merely accepting *their* distinctions and following *their* rules of logic, he was able to reduce the abhidharmists' theories to absurdities.

To assert that all distinctions are, in the final analysis, relative and interdependent is obviously different from *proving* they are so. This seemingly endless task was made manageable by Nāgārjuna's discovery of general principles applicable to each of the distinctions he encountered. T. R. V. Murti explains one of the most useful of these:

> Relation has to perform two mutually opposed functions: as *connecting* the two terms, in making them relevant to each other, it has to *identify* them; but as connecting the *two*, it has to *differentiate* them. Otherwise expressed, relation cannot obtain between entities that are identical with or different from each other.[2]

All philosophical systems discuss the relationships among certain key terms. In the abhidharma schools, for example, much analysis was directed at clarifying the precise relations among such concepts as cause and effect; past, present, and future; nirvana and illusion. Nāgārjuna recognized that each philosophical term serves as a distinction only vis-à-vis another term: no term exists *in vacuo*. One cannot have an understanding of cause without also having some understanding of effect, or change without stasis, or nirvana without illusion.

Nāgārjuna concludes that a philosophical system cannot assert the primacy of one term in any set without falling into serious paradoxes. If we know change is only meaningful insofar as it can be contrasted with stasis, for example, then the philosophical position that "all is change" (or its partner "all is stasis") is intrinsically problematic. How can one propound the universality of change if one's very understanding of change requires knowledge of something that does not exist (namely, stasis)? Stated differently, the original definitional interdependence of stasis–change is the domain within which the discussion of either stasis or change must take place. If the subsequent conclusion subverts the very relationship presupposed by the argument, the discussion itself becomes meaningless or, to use Nāgārjuna's term, empty *(śūnya)*.

To make this point more concrete, let us now consider two of Nāgārjuna's critiques from his *Mūlamadhyamakakārikā* [Fundamentals of the Middle Way], henceforth abbreviated *MK*.

## TWO NĀGĀRJUNAN CRITIQUES

*Time*

This easily grasped argument serves as a good introduction to Nāgārjuna's methodology. In *MK* 19, Nāgārjuna argues as follows:

1. If the existence of the present and future depends upon the past, then present and future should be in the past.
2. [For] if present and future were not there, how could present and future be dependent upon the past?
3. Moreover, without dependence upon the past, there is no occurrence of present and future. Thus present as well as future times would not exist.
4. In the same manner, the remaining two periods (of time), as well as (concepts such as) above, below, and middle, etc., or identity, etc., should be characterized.[3]

Nāgārjuna's point is that although many philosophical theories deal with the breakdown of time into past, present, and future, the relationship among these three terms is paradoxical. Each of the three terms is meaningful only in relation to the meanings of the other two. Yet, by the very definition of the terms, their referents (the past, the present, the future) never exist simultaneously. Therefore, the assumption that the terms *past*, *present*, and *future* refer to an objective reality outside language is absurd. Stated differently, if these terms refer to nonlinguistic bits of reality (as the abhidharmic philosophers had presumed), there can be no possible connection among those bits (since they never exist simultaneously)—and without those interconnections the terms themselves are meaningless. The conclusion is that it is absurd to think of the past, present, and future as having any extralinguistic reality.

## Causality

Nāgārjuna endeavored to undermine Indian (non-Buddhist as well as abhidharmic) arguments about causality by proving the relationship between cause and effect to be neither absolute nor unparadoxical. Specifically, in asserting that there really are causes and effects, one should be able to say whether or not the cause is philosophically identical with the effect. A common Indian logic recognizes four possible responses: cause and effect are (1) completely identical, (2) not at all identical, (3) both identical and not identical, (4) neither identical nor not identical. Nāgārjuna argues that each alternative leads to absurdity. Although his statements are extremely elliptical, we can propose the following reconstruction:

1. If the cause and effect are identical, then nothing different was caused or brought into existence. For there to be causality, something must *change*. If there is change, then the cause and effect cannot be identical. Thesis 1 is absurd. (See *MK* 1:5.)
2. Let us suppose that the cause (for simplicity of notation, call it $X$) and the effect $(Y)$ are not at all identical; that is, they are completely different. If so, there can be no *continuity* between $X$ and $Y$. Before $Y$ exists, there is only $X$; but $X$ cannot be considered the cause of something nonexistent, can it? After $Y$ comes into existence, why should we associate it exclusively with $X$ if they are completely different from each other? To hold to thesis 2 is to lose all connection between cause and effect and thereby to lose causality itself. Position 2 leads to absurdity. (See *MK* 1:6.)
3. Perhaps $X$ and $Y$ are somehow both identical and not identical. If $X$ and $Y$ are considered to be *unitary* entities, this is a patent contradiction in that $X = Y$ and *not* $(X = Y)$. If $X$ and $Y$ are *composite* entities, parts of which are identical and other parts different, where is the causal connection? If it is only in the identical parts, that is a reversion to position 1; if only in the nonidentical parts, that is a reversion to position 2. If the connection is necessarily in *both* the parts, then $X$ and $Y$ cannot be divisible entities insofar as they are in causal relations, and we

revert to $X = Y$ and *not (X = Y)*. Position 3 is absurd. (In *MK* 1:7, the conclusion is stated without argument. Presumably Nāgārjuna thought this position to be either a patent contradiction or a reversion to one of the previous positions. Both possibilities are reconstructed here.)

4. This leaves only one more possible view—that cause and effect are neither identical nor not identical—a position which apparently claims it is a misuse of language to apply the philosophical term *identical* to the relationship between cause and effect. If such a category mistake were indeed the case, however, all arguments about the identity of cause and effect would be meaningless—as meaningless as arguing, for example, whether the color of knowledge is red or not red. The preceding arguments have shown, however, that positions 1, 2, and 3 are meaningful though false. The reductio argument could not have been successful if the whole issue were merely an illusory semantic problem. Therefore, position 4 is shown to be absurd as well. (The conclusion, without argument, is stated in *MK* 1:7.)

Since all four possible answers yield absurdities, the bifurcation between cause and effect is itself suspect. Any theory assuming this distinction cannot avoid contradiction and paradox.

## THE IMPLICATIONS OF NĀGĀRJUNA'S THEORY OF EMPTINESS

What, then, is the gist of Nāgārjuna's enterprise? Conceptualization operates within certain relativistic limitations; no conceptual distinction has an absolute, totally objective, basis. When resorting to conceptualization, one must take a stand which, if analyzed in detail, can be shown to be limited in three ways. (1) Words cannot be assumed to be referents to nonlinguistic bits of reality. (2) No philosophical assertion based on conceptual distinctions can avoid an implicit acceptance of both of the opposing elements of the distinction. That is, any assertion of one side of a distinction over the other is, at its foundation, self-contradictory. (3) Any assertion or distinction only highlights one aspect of a situation and, in so doing, casts into shadows an equally important, though incompatible, aspect. Let us consider each point in turn.

First, as we have seen in our discussion of the Mādhyamikan critique of time in *MK* 19, linguistic distinctions do not necessarily refer to units of nonlinguistic reality. The epistemic use of a terminological distinction, or of a concept based on that distinction, does not necessarily mirror the way reality is ontically constructed. In this respect, Nāgārjuna rejects a strictly atomistic interpretation of language: the view that individual terms correspond one-to-one with bits of reality. Words are dependent on other words; concepts on other concepts. Nāgārjuna, in effect, moves from a picture theory of language to a language game theory, but he pushes this theory to its extreme conclusion. Insofar as they build systems out of conceptual distinctions referring merely to terminological interrelations, such philosophies lack connection with realities outside of language. That is to say, since language can never leave its own constructs and internal rules, it cannot serve as a vehicle for philosophical *truth*. Of course, language structures do overlap with structures found in our experience of concrete phenomena, but the overlap is fortuitous, not necessary. Therefore, language might serve us well in an everyday, pragmatic way, but for questions of ultimate philosophical and religious concern, it is altogether inadequate.

As for the second limitation of language, philosophy can be loosely defined as the enterprise of finding conceptual frameworks that interpret human experience (or, alternatively, reality) in a coherent, consistent, and communicable manner. Nāgārjuna's analysis implies that such an enterprise is doomed to failure. Insofar as philosophy relies on language for the formulation of its conceptual structures, it is forced to make distinctions that are ontologically arbitrary and misleading. With linguistic distinctions serving as its starting point, no philosophical assertion can be ultimate or unparadoxical. Let us consider the example of causality once again.

If we claim that "cause precedes effect," taking the phrase on face value, it seems so innocuous that most people would assent to it without hesitation. If we adopt a more critical attitude, however, its clarity is clouded by the interdependent (in Nāgārjuna's terms, empty) character of language. What, after all, *is* a cause? To define it, we must depend on the simultaneous characterization of its opposing partner, in this case effect. We cannot even conceive of a cause without thinking of its relation to effect. Therefore, there is something suspect in claiming that cause precedes effect. That is, in observing a series of events, we cannot see the prior event as a cause until we have also identified a succeeding event as an effect. Our labeling of cause and effect is simultaneous. Of course, Nāgārjuna does not argue from this observation that cause does not *really* precede effect. His overall argument is simply that our conceptual analysis of a situation is not a straightforward reflection of the way the situation is directly experienced. Concepts are *samvṛti*; they literally "cover" or "obstruct" the way things are actually experienced.[4] Thus, Nāgārjuna hopes to undercut the analytic and speculative philosophies of the abhidharma schools by showing that conceptual frameworks are not to be totally trusted.

In *MK*, Nāgārjuna attempts to demonstrate that none of the crucial terms of abhidharma (and much of Indian non-Buddhist) philosophy directly mirror the way things are experienced. There is an unbridgeable gap between the concepts and their supposed referents. Of course, there is nothing inappropriate about using the distinction between cause and effect in everyday life. Such distinctions are rough approximations useful in ordinary communication. The gap between such concepts and their referents is not so great that language is to be avoided entirely. Nāgārjuna's only claim is that since there *is* a gap, we can never reach reality through conceptual means alone.

This observation leads directly into the third limitation of language. In making a distinction, we claim that what had been taken to be an indivisible phenomenon is, in fact, a composite entity of at least two distinct parts. In other words, we take what had been one and divide it into two—for example, the growth of a tree is separated into the material cause and effect of acorn and oak. This process works well enough for many practical applications (in planting a tree farm, for example), but can we really *justify* the assumed relationship between the acorn and oak? To demonstrate how the two are related, we must return to the unitary view of the phenomenon: the growing of the tree. In other words, to show the rationale for their being distinguished, we must refer to the characterization in which they are not considered separate. Yet, as soon as we make that step, we can no longer show that they are distinguished.

In short, in analyzing any conceptual dichotomy, we fluctuate between two contradictory models (in this case, the growth of the tree versus the acorn/oak) which depend on each other for their definition; neither constitutes a satisfactory description in itself. This principle of interdependence is reminiscent of Murti's explanation of Nāgārjuna's principle of relation: every relation must perform the contradictory task of maintaining that the related entities are both completely identical and completely different.

Words in themselves, according to Nāgārjuna, are empty of independent reality: they exist as practical instruments for daily life. Their function is to highlight some aspect of a situation, but in so doing, they necessarily cast some other, equally real, aspect into the shadows. This does not, however, mean that no philosophical standpoint is better than any other. In Heidegger's terms, every assertion both conceals *and* reveals. We judge philosophies on the merits of what is revealed against what is concealed. Our criteria for this judgment are the philosophical interests and needs of our time and place.

## NĀGĀRJUNA'S EMPTINESS AND ZEN'S NOTHINGNESS

As noted at the beginning of this chapter, one of Zen's prominent characteristics is its mistrust of conceptual categories. Having examined Nāgārjuna's arguments for the relativity of philosophical distinctions, we have a new perspective on the openly contradictory nature of many Zen statements. Emptiness—the logical interdependence of opposing terms—lies at the basis of all philosophical distinctions. Still, it does not follow that one should abandon language altogether, transcending the world of dualities and living in the bliss of distinctionless trance states. As Streng observes,

Nāgārjuna believes one can operate within the world of duality while recognizing its relativity. In this regard, we should consider Nāgārjuna's emphasis on the nondifferentiating, nonobjectifying insight or wisdom known as *prajñā*.

*Prajñā*, a state of consciousness achieved through meditation, is not directly practical in dealing with the ordinary affairs of life, but it is invaluable in reinforcing the awareness that all ideas, their pragmatic usefulness notwithstanding, stand on emptiness *(śūn-yatā)*—a gap that conceptual thinking cannot span. Although the world itself is not illusory, our *characterizations* of the world are fundamentally self-contradictory, relative, and tentative. Without the insight of *prajñā*, we run the risk of becoming attached to our characterizations, of thinking of them as absolutes, rather than as names convenient for a given purpose. Streng summarizes how Nāgārjuna's logic leads to the traditional Buddhist concern for overcoming attachment:

> In practical life it is necessary to recognize that a chair is not a table, that a gold coin is not the same as clay, and that a merchant who cheats is not identical with one who does not. However, a person who does not slip into the error of regarding these practical distinctions as ultimate facts is able to see that there is indeed neither one absolute substance nor many individual substances. Every object of perception or imagination requires mental fabrication, and therefore every distinction participates in this fabrication. If, on the other hand, this distinction is accompanied by the assumption or conviction of an absolute reality, then psychic energies are stimulated which bind the person to the fabrication. It is this being bound to fabrication which is *saṁsāra* [illusion].[5]

Therefore, Streng argues,

> Nāgārjuna accepted the practical distinction between the two kinds of truth, and because this was only a practical distinction he felt free to use mundane truth, that required logical and semantic conventions, to dispel the attachment to the products of this truth and thereby lead the religious student toward Ultimate Truth.[6]

Now let us examine how the person is understood in Zen.

Like the modern Western personalists, Zen maintains that no characterization of the person ever captures its full reality: a description only highlights one aspect to the exclusion of others. Yet, unlike the personalists, the Zen tradition does not limit this principle to persons: any characterization of *anything* falls short in the same way. For Zen, this restriction is more important when it concerns the person only because human beings can delude themselves by identifying with particular descriptions. Dogs do not think of themselves as collies, spaniels, or even as dogs. Only humans reduce themselves to communists or capitalists, blacks or whites, centers of self-consciousness or of stimulus-response, disciples or Zen Masters. These categories are not intrinsically dangerous as long as one remembers them to be relative—that is, limited to specified perspectives. Once one starts to understand oneself or others as equivalent to these categories, however, one is closed to experiencing in ways inconsistent with the image. This is what Zen Buddhism considers the *attachment* to conceptualization. If one understands the relativity at the heart of all distinctions, consistency is not an excuse for dogmatism. For illustrative purposes, let us consider how a Zen Buddhist might respond to the Western controversy over the reality of personal essence.

For simplicity, let us take the essentialist view to be that there is a fixed characteristic distinguishing humans from all other beings and that the explication of this essence (or essences) is a basis for the description of any individual. On the one hand, there are Zen terms implying an essentialist standpoint. For example, we have seen that Zen recognizes the existence of a Buddha-nature, often interpreted to be the inherent potential for enlightenment. This potential, although it is possessed by all sentient beings, can be fully realized only by human beings. Another essentialist term is the original face the Zen student is challenged to present; that is, one is required to manifest what one is, outside of all physical and historical conditions. On the other hand, as we might expect, Zen sometimes takes the opposite view also. Not only does it deny the reality of personal ego; it also denies that anything substantive or unchanging exists at all: everything is impermanent. Before this chapter, we might have despaired over the apparent inconsistency, but now, owing to Nāgārjuna, we see a rationale behind what seems to be a flagrant suspension of logic.

From Nāgārjuna's standpoint, the distinction between personal essence or no personal essence is only a relative one; to advocate either one to the exclusion of the other results in paradox. If we maintain that there is a fixed essence, for example, then we would have to say that the person as person—that is, the person as fixed essence—cannot change. Without personal change, there is no personal growth or personal agency and we lose hold of the person in every ordinary sense of the word. Suppose, then, we claim that there is no fixed essence at all. In that case, what is to prevent a person from changing into a cow or a horse? By losing what makes the person distinguishable, we have again lost the person. Compared with these absurdities, the Zen Masters' nonsense looks more like common sense: the inconsistency of maintaining both views seems less objectionable than the absurdity of maintaining either view exclusively.

We may compare this Zen attitude with the way we ordinarily use such imprecise modes of expression as diagrams, analogies, metaphors, and models. We do not require completeness of a diagram or analogy: they are intended merely to isolate certain relationships or to emphasize certain aspects. Nor do we necessarily insist on consistency: since these modes of expression communicate a specific point of information, we assume there to be differences in expression when other points are considered. We might, for example, have two maps of the United States: a roadmap showing the geographical location and size of the states and a map representing the size of the states proportional to their number of electoral votes. If we look at the comparative sizes of, say, North Dakota and Connecticut, the representations are seemingly inconsistent. On the first map, North Dakota is fourteen times larger than Connecticut; on the other, Connecticut is almost three times larger than North Dakota. Since the two maps have different purposes, however, we accept the inconsistency as not only necessary but helpful. We use one map to plan a vacation trip, the other to plan a presidential campaign strategy. We might even use *both* in planning a series of campaign speeches.

Nāgārjuna and his Zen descendants maintain that critical argumentation is no more precise than these other modes of expression.

The philosophical distinction between personal essence and no essence, for example, merely presents two alternative models. For Zen, completeness and consistency are not as critical as the intended use and appropriateness of the model. Therefore, when it furthers his aims, the Zen Master may speak as if there is a personal essence; when it is more helpful to deny this essence, he will do so with as much aplomb as the campaign manager shifting his attention from one map to the other.

Certain utterances of the Zen Masters now become more intelligible. We may still find them contradictory or paradoxical, but we know the sense in which *all* utterances share that quality if we push analysis of them far enough. We are now ready to look beyond what the Zen Master says or does—to the *source* of his actions. Remember that the master not only perceives *mu* ("nothingness"); he *is* it. This ontological language is still strange. We have seen that nothingness is the relativity or emptiness at the ground of thought, that the very analysis of language and thought is a maelstrom, pulling us down into nothingness. But we have yet to see how nothingness emanates outward toward us, beckoning us to return to the very source of all existence. To understand this aspect of nothingness, we turn to the characterization of Nonbeing found in Chinese Taoism.

As we leave our discussion of language, let us take one final glance through the eyes of Bashō, a Zen Buddhist lay disciple and one of Japan's most admired poets. In this haiku, he expresses the Zen qualms about putting things into words. There is no argument or justification: only the expression of a feeling, a sense of loss. If we listen carefully to the silence between the second and third lines, we hear the beckoning whisper of nothingness:

| | |
|---|---|
| *Mono ieba* | Whenever something is said, |
| *Kuchibiru samushi* | The lips are cold. |
| *Aki no kaze.*[7] | The autumn wind. |

# CHAPTER 3

# Chinese Taoism: The Pre-ontology of Nonbeing

In the preceding chapter we investigated the first of the two strands of the Zen doctrine of nothingness: the mistrust of conceptualization. Here we consider the second strand: nothingness as *source*. For maximum clarity, we again step outside the Zen tradition itself, this time to investigate the pre-Zen standpoint of Chinese Taoist philosophy, primarily the writings of Lao Tzŭ and Chuang Tzŭ.[1] Their works, the *Tao Tê Ching* and the *Chuang Tzŭ*, are the cornerstones of the Taoist tradition and in them we find the initial identification of Nonbeing with the source of all things. Although the Zen doctrine of nothingness typically affirms this identification without detailed argument, Lao Tzŭ and Chuang Tzŭ attempt to explicate and justify it in a philosophically persuasive manner.

## THE ABSOLUTE AND THE RELATIVE TAO

First, we investigate the term *tao* itself ("way, path; to give an account"),[2] especially the fact that it is used in two seemingly disparate ways. On the one hand, it arbitrarily names the ultimate, ineffable principle. On the other hand, it refers to the creative function, a reflection or product of something more fundamental. Let us consider each of these uses in turn.

### Tao as Ineffable Absolute

Lao Tzŭ opens the *Tao Tê Ching* with the famous lines:

> The *Tao* that can be spoken of is not the *Tao* itself.
> The name that can be given is not the name itself.[3]

This passage points to an ineffable ground of all existence—to that which eludes our grasp as soon as we point it out or give it a name. The Chinese term for "*Tao* itself" is *ch'ang tao*; the *ch'ang* signifies permanence and constancy. We will call this the absolute Tao, the term *absolute* referring to the claim that this Tao is uncontradictable. As CH'ĒNG Hao (1032–1085) pithily put it, "The Tao has no opposite."[4]

We find references to this absolute Tao throughout the writings of Chuang Tzŭ and Lao Tzŭ. For example, Chuang Tzŭ speaks of Tao as beyond any dichotomy between *this* and *that:*

> Therefore the sage does not proceed in such a way [seeing things in opposition], but illuminates all in the light of Heaven. He too recognizes a "this," but a "this" which is also "that," a "that" which is also "this." His "that" has both a right and a wrong in it; his "this" too has both a right and a wrong in it. So, in fact, does he still have a "this" and "that"? A state in which "this" and "that" no longer find their opposites is called the hinge of the Way [Tao].[5]

As for the arbitrariness of the name Tao in referring to the ineffable absolute, Lao Tzŭ writes in chap. 25:

> Silent! Empty!
> Existing by itself, unchanging,
> Pervading everywhere, inexhaustible,
> It might be called the mother of the world.
> Its name is unknown;
> I simply call it *Tao.*
> If I were to exert myself to define it,
> I might call it great.

## Tao as a Dependent, Creative Function

Despite the preceding descriptions of Tao as primary, Lao Tzŭ also speaks as if it were dependent on, or "in accord with" *(fa)*, something else. He is most explicit in the same chap. 25:

> Man is in accordance with earth.
> Earth is in accordance with heaven.
> Heaven is in accordance with *Tao.*
> *Tao* is in accordance with that which is.

Hence Tao is not simply self-contained and permanent; it is dependent, in this case, on "that which is." In other places, the preferred term is *wu* (in Japanese, *mu*), commonly translated as "Nonbeing" to suggest the ontological dimension of Taoism. Let us examine two juxtaposed passages:

> From the *Tao*, one is created;
> From one, two;
> From two, three;
> From three, ten thousand things. [chap. 42]

> Ten thousand things in the universe are created from being.
> Being is created from non-being. [chap. 40]

When understood as a procreative force, Tao is apparently equivalent to, or at least a part of, Being. In this sense, however, Tao is no longer the self-sufficient, absolute Tao; it is dependent on something more fundamental—namely, what Lao Tzŭ here calls "nonbeing." In his development of the Taoist tradition, Chuang Tzŭ elaborates on Lao Tzŭ's suggestion and explicitly makes Nonbeing the primordial category:

> In the Great Beginning, there was nonbeing; there was no being, no name. Out of it arose One; there was One, but it had no form. Things got hold of it and came to life, and it was called Virtue [*tê*, close in meaning to the Latin *virtus*, implying both essential strength and moral excellence]. Before things had forms, they had their allotments; these were of many kinds, but not cut off from one another, and they were called fates. Out of the flow and flux, things were born, and as they grew they developed distinctive shapes; these were called forms.[6]

In this description of Nonbeing as primal and nameless, Chuang Tzŭ has, in effect, made Nonbeing an equivalent for the absolute Tao *(ch'ang tao)*. Kaltenmark, too, takes this interpretation:

> Chuang Tzu and Lao Tzu are thus imagining something anterior to Chaos (the One); a kind of absolute void that Chuang Tzu calls the *wu* [Nonbeing] and Lao Tzu the *tao*. This Tao is thus the *ch'ang tao* of [Lao Tzŭ's] Chapter I, and the One is the equivalent of the "*tao* that can be named."[7]

Two points essential to our investigation of Tao and Nonbeing can now be identified. First, Tao is used in two senses. On the one hand, it is an arbitrary name for the ineffable absolute—that is, for what is beyond distinctions and oppositions. On the other hand, it refers to a cosmogonic force dependent on something else, this something else being variously called the *ch'ang tao*, the "that which is," or Nonbeing. Second, the term Nonbeing, in Chuang Tzŭ especially, is elevated to the primary position normally occupied by the absolute Tao, and in this usage the term is an arbitrary name for the nameless and formless.

## BEING AND NONBEING IN TAOISM

As the equivalent of the absolute Tao, Nonbeing or nothingness (Chinese *wu*; Japanese *mu*) is more than the mere opposite of Being. It is in fact ontologically *prior* to Being; it is the ultimate source of all things. As Wing-tsit CHAN remarks, this property makes it essentially positive rather than negative:

> On the surface non-being seems to be empty and devoid of everything. Actually, this is not the case. It is devoid of limitations but not devoid of definite characteristics. . . . Tao as non-being, then, is not negative but positive in character. This concept of non-being was absolutely new in Chinese thought and most radical. Other Chinese schools of thought conceived of non-being simply as the absence of something, but in Taoism it is only positive; it is basic.[8]

Because Nonbeing is prior to Being, however, we should not infer it to have an ontic value of its own. As the ineffable fountainhead of all existence, it *precedes* and underlies the distinction between Being and its opposite, Nonbeing. For this reason, it is perhaps best to speak in terms of a *pre*-ontology of Nonbeing, for it would be absurd to say that Nonbeing *exists*. By personifying the concepts, Chuang Tzŭ makes this point in an amusing fashion:

> Bright Dazzlement asked Non-existence, "Sir, do you exist or do you not exist?" Unable to obtain any answer, Bright Dazzlement stared intently at the other's face and form—all was vacuity and blankness. He

stared all day but could see nothing, listened but could hear no sound, stretched out his hand but grasped nothing. "Perfect!" exclaimed Bright Dazzlement. "Who can reach such perfection? I can conceive of the existence of nonexistence, but not of the nonexistence of nonexistence. How could I ever reach such perfection!"[9]

To ontologize Nonbeing, to consider it an entity, is a mistake. While we may be able to conceive of Nonbeing only through the aid of such an ontologization, its very conceivability proves it is not true Nonbeing, true *ch'ang tao*. To make Nonbeing effable is to rob it of its only distinguishing characteristic.

On the other hand, we have also seen that Lao Tzŭ and Chuang Tzŭ state unequivocally that Nonbeing is the source of Being. This is paradoxical, for to speak of Nonbeing as the source of Being is, in some respect, to define and characterize that Nonbeing. If Nonbeing has a describable function (creating Being), it is no longer indeterminate but is describable precisely to the extent that it does something specific. Thus, we are left with the prospect of either denying Nonbeing's ineffability or denying its functionality; the two characteristics seem mutually exclusive.

Obviously, the term Nonbeing has both absolute and relative senses parallel to those of Tao. If this is the case, we are left with the problem of characterizing the precise relationship between the absolute and relative senses of Nonbeing. How can something be at once incontrovertible and related to its opposite? As the primal principle and source, Nonbeing must be originally without opposite and, at the same time, capable of interrelation with Being. As a key to understanding the Taoist view, we now resort to an extended analogy.

## THE ALLEGORY OF THE BELL

Walking along a mountain path in Japan, we come upon a rudimentary hermitage with a large temple bell suspended from a simple wooden pagoda. Unlike Western carillon bells, the Japanese bell has no clapper and is struck on the outside much as one might strike a gong (in this case by a small log suspended from the pagoda by two ropes). Admiring the excellence and obvious age of the engravings on the casting, we hear the footsteps of the temple priest and turn to ask, "How old is this extraordinary bell?" Touching his palm to the massive casting, he responds, "This is about five hundred years old, but" (removing his hand to point into the black void within the bell) "the emptiness within—*that's* eternal." He then proceeds to swing the striker gently back and forth, holding it lightly, but firmly, with his two hands. Almost indiscernibly he releases it, letting it swing freely so that it strikes the metal casting. The even tone permeates the area from the distant mountains across the valley, beyond the tops of the cedars, back to the very foundations of the hermitage. It seems as if the bell had rung itself, as if even the leaves stopped rustling in the wind to attend to its music. Smiling, the priest looks at us and asks, "Now please answer *my* question. Where did the sound come from—from the metal casting or from the emptiness inside?" Taken aback, we are dumbfounded. Still smiling, the monk turns, walking back to his hermitage.

To refine the analogy, think of the casting of the bell as Being and the hollow center as Nonbeing. The bell's function, the ringing of its unique tonal quality, is located neither in the casting nor in its emptiness. Without the hollow interior, the bell would be a metal slab that might clang but certainly could never emit music. On the other hand, the hollowness without the casting could only produce the rushing echo of silence. For the bell to resound, both the Being and the Nonbeing of the bell are necessary. From this point of view, the hermit was right to point out the limitation of our question. We mistook the bell to be only its metal casting, but the bell is *both* the casting *and* the emptiness within.

Let us look more closely at this emptiness. It truly *is* eternal, unlike the metal casting which will eventually corrode away. Even when the metal has completely disappeared, the space, the Nonbeing that had been enclosed in that bell will, in a sense, still exist. Although no longer the determinate space-within-the-bell, it will return to the boundless, infinite space from which it had been originally delimited when the bell was cast. The space within the bell's enclosure is in itself the same regardless of whether the bell encloses

it or not, but for that period of time in which it is enclosed by the
bell, its relatedness to the casting makes it *functional:* vibrating in
unison with the metal casting, it can ring. Furthermore, when that
emptiness is released from the enclosure of the bell, it loses its
specificity and its unique meaning. It is no longer identifiable; it
becomes nameless once again.

We can now return to our initial question: what do the Taoists
mean in asserting that Nonbeing is the source of Being? As already
observed, Nonbeing itself is timeless and unchanging; only through
its interrelatedness with Being does it become specific, determinate,
and meaningful. Analogous to the way all existence takes place
within the context of space, all Being abides within Nonbeing.
It should be remembered, though, that Nonbeing has no ontic
reality of its own. This is why we refer to Nonbeing itself as *pre-
ontological;* that is, it neither exists nor does it not exist.

Returning to the analogy, if we consider what that boundless,
infinite space is in and of itself (without its relations to entities), we
find that it is nothing. Space itself is nonexistent; things *in* space exist. We cannot even say that space is empty, since that implies a
relation to something else that is not there; empty implies empty of
*something.* Despite its nothingness, however, space is potentiality.
There can be no physical things without it. The existent requires
space for its arena, and space requires existents to transform it
from nothing into something specific—that is, to transform it from
the ineffable, timeless *that which has no name* into the specifically
meaningful here (contrasted with there). Similarly, Nonbeing is an
empty potentiality until it interpenetrates with Being, *giving birth
to all things.* But as soon as it does, as soon as it becomes delimited
and specifically meaningful, it is no longer absolute. In effect, by
becoming speakable, it falls into the relativity of Nāgārjuna's
*śūnyatā;* Nonbeing becomes dependent on Being for its very meaning. Without Being, Nonbeing lacks all definite signification.

Only by understanding Nonbeing as *both* absolute and relative
can we understand how it is the source of Being. If we think of
Nonbeing only in its relative sense, it is the mere contrary of Being.
If we think of it only in its absolute sense, it is self-contained and
ineffable. By following the interpretation suggested by the allegory

of the bell, however, we can make sense of this Taoist interweaving of Being and Nonbeing, the formed and the formless. We will have occasion much later to refer again to the bell and to the hermit's comments, but having accomplished our immediate purpose of clarifying the basic principle in the Taoist doctrine of Nonbeing, let us now see how it applies to Zen.

## TAOIST NONBEING AND ZEN NOTHINGNESS

As a metaphysical, cosmogonic principle, the Taoist Nonbeing is of only marginal interest to Zen. But Taoism also has practical concerns. Like Zen it has an interest in the nature of human experience. In fact, cosmogony is only a preface to its major focus: the proper manner of living in a world structured by those principles. The Way *(tao)* is not only the way the world functions, but also the way to lead one's life. For the Taoist, personal creativity is a microcosm of the structures we have just now been discussing. In other words, just as Nonbeing is the source of Being, so there is an inner, indeterminate core of creativity within the person as well. The Taoist's activity, like the operation of the Tao itself, arises naturally *in accordance with that which is.* To objectify the self, to consider it an agent of activity, is to overlook the Nonbeing at the source of all existence.

Thus, the Taoist ideal of personal activity, *wu-wei* or "non-doing," is an unselfconscious responsiveness. The Taoist endeavors not to interfere with the patterns of change, but to contemplate and be harmonious with them as they are enacted. To exert oneself in direct confrontation with any situation always meets with resistance, so Lao Tzŭ advises us to be like water—responsive and yielding, but not in a passive or fatalistic way. By yielding, the water follows its path and eventually wears away the rock obstructing it. In chap. 43 of the *Tao Tê Ching,* Lao Tzŭ remarks:

> The meekest in the world
> Penetrates the strongest in the world
> As nothingness enters into that-which-has-no-opening.
> Hence, I am aware of the value of non-action *[wu-wei]*

And of the value of teaching with no words;
As for the value of non-action,
Nothing in the world can match it.

That is, the Taoist acts as the Tao itself functions: creating through the interplay of Nonbeing and Being. By bringing nothing of one's own to one's activity, by remaining what Lao Tzŭ calls the "uncarved block" *(p'o)*, the Taoist "enters into that-which-has-no-opening." Through meditation and self-discipline, one learns to empty oneself—to eliminate all conscious striving and become truly spontaneous and responsive to the flow of events.[10] Lao Tzŭ writes in chap. 16:

Contemplate the ultimate void.
Remain truly in quiescence.
All things are together in action,
But I look into their non-action.
Things are unceasingly moving and restless,
Yet each one is proceeding back to the origin.
Proceeding back to the origin is quiescence.
To be in quiescence is to return to the destiny of being *[ming]*.

It is here that Taoism's Nonbeing most closely relates to Zen's nothingness. Both the Zen Buddhist and the Taoist try to return to the source of personhood: the inner nondiscriminating, nonbifurcating core, the basis of all discrimination. While the Taoists see this return as modeled on metaphysical and cosmological principles, Zen is primarily interested not in the source of the universe, but in the source of our experience of the universe. In this way, Zen weaves together the two strands of nothingness, for the origin of experience is where linguistic distinctions (and the concepts based on them) have not yet arisen. Through this synthesis, Zen Buddhism simultaneously undertakes both Nāgārjuna's project of overcoming our dependence on conceptualization and Taoism's project of becoming grounded in the nondiscriminating source of the person. In the next chapter, we examine more closely how this interweaving is actually achieved.

Before continuing, let us pause a moment with our companion Bashō. The sun is setting, casting its last glimmer on the aging poet, seated on a rock at the mountain temple of Ryūshaku-ji. He has spent the afternoon climbing along the cliffs, visiting the various subtemples, burning a stick or two of incense, offering a prayer. Exhausted, he is nonetheless caught up in the tranquillity and solitude of the place. Picking up his brush, he writes a haiku into his diary:

*Shizukasa ya*      Ah, the stillness!
*Iwa ni shimiiru*     Penetrating into the rocks
*Semi no koe.*[11]     A cicada's chirp.

Here we find a perfect example of the form of the formless: the blending of the distinctionless silence with the distinctive presence of the insect's chirp.

# CHAPTER 4

# No-Mind: The Zen Response to Nothingness

The last two chapters examined the two major strands out of which Zen weaves its conception of nothingness. Nāgārjuna's *śūnyatā* ("emptiness") is primarily a critique of philosophical distinctions whereas the Taoist pre-ontology of *wu* ("Nonbeing") emphasizes an indeterminate, distinctionless reality, the origin of all things, including human action. In this chapter we demonstrate how these two traditions contribute to what we have called the *context* of the person in Zen.

One of the first points to note about the Zen view of nothingness is that the Japanese language (like Chinese) formally distinguishes between Nāgārjuna's emptiness and Taoism's Nonbeing. *Śūnyatā* is technically translated as *kū* (*k'ung* in Chinese), and the Chinese *wu* is changed only in pronunciation into the Japanese *mu*. In Chinese and Japanese Buddhist history, these two words received various interpretations, sometimes being considered almost synonymous, sometimes quite distinct.[1] Without delving into historical complexities, we may assume that if the Zen tradition had wanted to maintain a clear-cut distinction between the two terms, it was at least linguistically possible to do so. This is not what happened. Particularly in modern Japanese Rinzai Zen Buddhist practice, *mu* has become the primary term, often used nontechnically to include the meaning of *kū* as well. This is why we must sometimes distinguish the word *mu* as Taoism's Nonbeing from *mu* in its wider sense of Zen's nothingness—an idea including Nāgārjuna's emptiness as well as Taoism's Nonbeing. It is this wider application of *mu* which shapes the distinctively Zen context of the person.

## *MU* AS CONTEXT OF THE ZEN PERSON

As we saw in Chapter 1, the individual *(kojin)* in Japan is merely an object selected out of a group; it is independent of all social, economic, and familial relationships. In effect, one is incommunicado with the rest of society. There is no human interaction, indeed no sense of self-esteem since this requires the support of others for reinforcement. When located within a social nexus, however, that individual acquires meaning as a human being *(ningen)*. Through one's betweenness—the relatedness to others and to components of society transcending one's individuality—one has a place in the world, an identity as a person *(ningen)*. Within a specific set of relationships, the person has obligations of respect to those above and obligations of responsibility to those below.[2] The epitome of bilateral duty has traditionally been the family: the relations between parents and children, husband and wife, older and younger siblings, male and female. Even the relationships between in-laws is governed to some extent by the relative social stature of the families involved.

This social identity is stripped away when one enters the monastery or nunnery. Giving up all possessions except those which can be carried in a little box suspended by a strap from the neck, the novitiate is literally given a new name and the head is shaved. (Hairstyle was traditionally a distinguishing mark of aristocratic and samurai families.) One is thus removed from one's former social place; formal ties with the family are broken and the self-definition gained therefrom is erased. Suddenly the Zen novitiate is alone, alone in a way unknown in the West, where identity is as much individual as social. The novitiate naturally seeks new structures, new parameters to help determine who and what he or she is.

In certain respects the monastery quickly fills this vacuum. As in secular frameworks, there is a clear hierarchical order: the Zen Master at the top, followed by a few senior monks in charge of everyday details, on down to the newest member of the community. Strict projects affect almost every moment of the monk's day from before dawn to nine or ten at night. Besides the daily meditation periods, about once a month a *sesshin* is held: an entire week is spent solely in meditation (except for meals, an occasional lecture, and minimal activities necessary for personal maintenance). Eating a vegetarian diet for bare subsistence, begging for food, and physically laboring in the fields, kitchen, or laundry, the monk would seem to have neither the energy nor the time for an identity crisis.

On the other hand, the Zen monastery does not erase a personal identity merely to sketch a new one over it. The new monk's life is designed to be paradoxical and problematic. Presumably, the monk has entered the monastery, has rent the very fabric of his former identity, in order to achieve enlightenment or satori. Yet questions about the nature of this enlightenment, or even requests for instruction in how to achieve it, are typically ignored or rebuffed:

> Once a monk made a request of Joshu. "I have just entered the monastery," he said. "Please give me instructions, Master." Joshu said, "Have you had your breakfast?" "Yes, I have," replied the monk. "Then," said Joshu, "wash the bowls." The monk had an insight.[3]

That is, although the monk had entered the monastery with a specific goal in mind (to receive instruction; to achieve satori), that purpose was transformed into *no*-purpose, his longings into *no*-longings, his goal into *no*-goal.

Devoid as it is of any formal rationale, the Zen life is qualitatively different from any previous way of life. *Mu* or nothingness is a universal solvent. Not only does it dissolve any conceptualization trying to grasp it, but, even more radically, it dissolves itself. It is like a dim star in the evening sky: it disappears when one tries to focus on it, but as soon as one gives up that focus, one sees it peripherally, knowing it to have been there all along. Consequently, the *no* of no-purpose, no-longings, and no-goal is not really a negation; like *mu* itself, it is something *prior* to either affirmation or negation. Commenting on the command to "wash the bowls," Shibayama says, "For Joshu, to live Zen was not to lead a Zen-like life;

but to live an ordinary life, just as it is, was Zen."[4] Even within the
Sōtō branch of Zen, where training by koans and paradoxical
stories is minimized, monks or nuns who ask *why* they are to sit (in
meditation) are told not to "sit to meditate" but to "sit to sit."

Consequently, the *mu* is not like other contexts at all; it is
without a specifiable content. The more one allows oneself to be
defined by the monastery, the more one's determinate personhood
is taken away. In the Rinzai tradition, during periods of intense
meditation *(sesshin)*, the monk may have to present himself before
the Zen Master as often as four times a day. Each time the monk
is given rationally insoluble puzzles to which one must respond,
puzzles such as: "Show me your original face before your parents
were born" or "What is the sound of one hand [clapping]?" or
Shibayama's "I want to see that form which has no-form." As
Shibayama explains, "The secret of Zen lies in this really throwing
oneself away."[5] The Sōtō Zen Master Dōgen called this the "molting of body-mind." No wonder the monks in the Rinzai temple
often have to be dragged forcibly into the Zen Master's chambers
for another interview. Further effort at solving puzzles leads to the
further eroding of the sense of self one cherishes. In chap. 48 of the
*Tao Tê Ching* are the famous lines:

> To learn,
> One accumulates day by day.
> To study Tao,
> One reduces day by day.

Every day in the monastery, the Zen disciple learns to throw away
a little more of the self.

What exactly is the *purpose* of this training? Have we no alternative but to call it the purpose of no-purpose and leave it at that?
Although we cannot see the electron with our naked eyes, we can
follow its trail in a cloud chamber—in like manner, although we
can never focus directly on the purpose of Zen training, we can
nevertheless trace its path. In characterizing Jōshū's demand to
"wash the bowls," Shibayama gives us a trail marker: "It is nothing but asking you to live with no-mind, which can be attained
only after long, sincere, and assiduous striving."[6]

## NO-MIND: THE RESPONSE TO *MU*

The Japanese characters for the term *no-mind* are the now familiar
*MU* ("no" or "nothingness") and the character *SHIN* (*kokoro:*
"mind, spirit, heart"). Thus, no-mind also has the connotations of
*mu*-spirit or *mu*-consciousness. The term *no-mind* is historically
related to the "no-thought" *(munen)* that Enō (Ch: Hui-nêng), the
sixth Chinese Zen patriarch, calls the main doctrine of Zen:

> Good friends, in this teaching of mine, from ancient times up to the
> present, all have set up no-thought as the main doctrine, non-form as
> the substance and non-abiding as the basis. Non-form is to be sep-
> arated from form even when associated with form. No-thought is not
> to think even when involved in thought. Non-abiding is the original
> nature of man.[7]

Enō's three technical terms all begin with the character *mu* (*wu*
in Chinese): "no-thought" (Ch: *wu-nien*; Jp: *munen*), "non-form"
(Ch: *wu-hsiang*; Jp: *musō*), "non-abiding" (Ch: *wu-chu*; Jp: *mujū*).
In Enō's characterization, *mu* is again not a simple negation: non-
form is still associated with form, and no-thought occurs even when
one is involved in thought. But what does it mean to be at once in
thinking and no-thought? Enō continues:

> Successive thoughts do not stop; prior thoughts, present thoughts, and
> future thoughts follow one after the other without cessation. If one
> instant of thought is cut off, the Dharma body [here meaning the
> transindividual identification with all of reality] separates from the
> physical body, and in the midst of successive thoughts there will be no
> place for attachment to anything. If one instant of thought clings,
> then successive thoughts cling; this is known as being fettered. If in
> all things successive thoughts do not cling, then you are unfettered.
> Therefore, non-abiding is made the basis.[8]

Here Enō draws an explicit connection between no-thought and
nonabiding. One of the fundamental concepts of Indian Buddhism
is *pratītya samutpāda:* the conditional or causal interdependence of
all things. Here this principle is applied to the interrelatedness of
the succession of thoughts: an attitude of attachment in one
moment continues to influence the following moments unless there

is an effort to break the series. This attachment may assume myriad forms. For example, the Early Buddhists saw it as "craving" (Skrt: *tṛṣṇā;* Pali: *taṇhā*)—in particular, craving for the permanence of either desired objects or the self. In other words, attachment was seen as the attempt to *hold onto* desired things and to see the self as an unchanging, eternal essence rather than the locus of a virtually infinite number of conditioning processes. This doctrine of the lack of permanent self or soul—that is, the rejection of the self as an independent agent separate from the web of interconnected conditioned causes—is called in Sanskrit the doctrine of *anātman* ("no-ego"; *anattā* in Pali, *muga* in Japanese). The doctrine of no-mind is really an extension of this idea.

This does not mean that consciousness itself is denied. A modern Chinese Zen Master explains:

> The so-called No-mind . . . is not like clay, wood, or stone, that is, utterly devoid of consciousness; nor does the term imply that the mind stands still without any reaction when it contacts objects or circumstances in the world. It does not adhere to anything, but is natural and spontaneous at all times and under all circumstances. There is nothing impure within it; neither does it remain in a state of impurity. When one observes his body and mind, he sees them as magic shadows or as a dream. Nor does he abide in this magic and dreamlike state. . . . When he reaches this point, then he can be considered as having arrived at the true state of No-mind.[9]

The person of no-mind sees the objects of the world as neither real nor unreal, as neither independent substances nor dreams or illusions. Here, then, lies the connection between no-thought and nonform: without denying the forms encountered in daily life, the Zen Buddhist, nonetheless, does not cling to them or take them to be the only reality.

In a similar vein, UCHIYAMA Kōshō, a contemporary Zen Master of the Sōtō branch, tries to express the relationship between thinking and zazen (seated Zen meditation):

> Here we must clearly distinguish "thinking" and "chasing after thoughts" from "thoughts occurring." If during zazen a thought occurs to you and you chase after it, then you're already thinking and

not doing zazen. But this doesn't mean that you're doing zazen only
when thoughts have entirely ceased to occur. . . .
     Even if you take a stationary position like the rock, you can't say
that, like the rock, no thoughts will occur to you. Moreover, if
thoughts did cease to occur to you, we would have to say that you
weren't alive. . . . Therefore, it's false that thoughts cease to occur to a
person sitting zazen, rather it's natural that thoughts should occur.
But, if a person chases after thoughts, he is thinking and no longer
doing zazen. So what should our attitude be?
     . . . When we think, we think of "something." Thinking of "some-
thing" means grasping that something with thought. But during zazen
we open wide the hand of thought which is trying to grasp something,
and don't grasp at anything at all. This is "letting go of thoughts."
     Actually, maybe some thought will occur to you. But if only the
thought does not grasp, it will not be formed into any "thing." For
example, even if thought A (a flower) occurs to you, as long as it is
not followed by thought B (is beautiful) no significance such as A is B
(a flower is beautiful) is formed. Neither is it something which could
be taken in the sense of A which is B (beautiful flower). Then, even if
thought A does occur in your head, as long as you don't continue the
thought, A stands before the formation of meaning. It is meaningless,
and in that condition will disappear as consciousness flows on.[10]

Because of past conditioning, certain naming activities are inevit-
able. Even in a state of deep meditation, the word *doorbell* might
pop into mind when its ring is abruptly heard. Yet, Uchiyama
claims, thought can be let go at precisely that point. No further
judgmental or analytic process need occur—and without that
judgmental moment, real meaning, in his full sense of the word,
does not arise. Thus, no-mind is really nothingness-mind insofar as
it is, in Uchiyama's terms, "before the formation of meaning." The
mind is, so to speak, suspended in a state preceding the bestowal of
meaning. This state is described by the Taoist as the source of
Being and Nonbeing or the form of the formless.
     To sum up, all three of these concepts—no-thought (or no-mind),
nonabiding, and nonform—hover around the same point: the characterization of a state of consciousness that does not progress in the
usual diachronic, linear way, one thought emerging out of its
predecessor. Rather, the content of each experienced moment forms

the content of that moment's thought. This notion may seem tautological, but there is an implicit distinction here between what might be labeled "nonconceptualized experience" and "thought":

> Coming to a ford in a river, two Zen monks met a beautiful maiden who asked assistance in getting across because of the depth and strength of the current. The first monk hesitated, starting to make apologies—the rules of the religious order forbade physical contact with women. The second monk, on the other hand, without a moment's hesitation picked her up and carried her across. With a parting gesture of thanks, the young woman continued on her way, the two monks going off in the other direction. After some time, the first monk said to the second, "You shouldn't have picked her up like that—the rules forbid it." The second monk replied in surprise, "You must be very tired indeed! As soon as we had crossed the river I put her down. But you! You have been carrying her all this time!"[11]

The irony, of course, is this: although he did not carry the woman physically, the first monk was fixed on the *idea* of the woman. Unable to respond to her sincere request for help, he saw her only as a potential threat to his monastic purity. In fact, the first monk's ratiocination merely presented him with a further problem: how to deal with the second monk's violation of the rules of the order. The second monk, on the other hand, brought nothing to the encounter with the woman and left it with nothing. He acted in a state of no-mind, responding without hesitation to the evident need of another person. Restating the difference between the two, the first monk understood himself only in terms of the category *monk*, seeing the person before him merely in terms of the category *woman*. He was, therefore, entangled in determining the proper interrelations between *woman* and *monk*. While the first monk was paralyzed by these considerations, the second monk had already picked up the woman and left her behind. While the first monk was thinking about the past and future, the second monk was acting in the present without a linked series of conceptualizations.

The second monk's mind was not completely passive, of course. No-mind is still a functioning mind, as we see in this dialogue between a student and his master, NAN'YŌ Echū (Ch: NAN-YANG Hui-chung), himself a disciple of Enō:

Student:  Having already attained the state of absolute no-ness, one is
          perfect master of oneself; but how would you use the mind
          (yung-hsin), when hunger and cold assail you?
Master:   When hungry, I eat, and when cold I put on more clothes.
Student:  If you are aware of hunger and cold, you have a mind (yu-
          hsin) [opposite of wu-hsin, no-mind].
Master:   I have a question for you: Has the mind you speak of as a
          mind (yu-hsin hsin) a form?
Student:  The mind has no form.
Master:   If you already knew that the mind has no form, that means
          that from the first the mind is not, and how could you talk
          about having a mind?[12]

That is, although the mind may function, it does not necessarily
have a form, making it a substantive thing. Following Nāgārjuna,
it is unjustifiable to see *any* concept, even no-mind, as a perfect
reflection of a nonlinguistic entity—that is, as absolute. No-mind
must be directly manifested; as soon as it is objectified and transformed into a conscious goal, it is lost.

To restate these points, no-mind or no-thought is a state of consciousness in which the dichotomy between subject and object,
experiencer and experienced, is overcome. Avoiding the usual
categories imposed on experience (the flower is beautiful, a monk
cannot have contact with a woman, or whatever), the function of
no-mind is to respond immediately to present experiential data. Insofar as it withdraws from active intellectualization, this function
of no-mind can be considered a passive state, but it is also active in
two senses. First, this withdrawal requires, at least initially, an act
of the will. As Enō said in his analysis of nonabiding, the attitude
of clutching at dearly held thoughts will be carried over from one
thought-moment to the next unless one makes an *effort* to break the
chain. (Of course, in one sense, this activity cannot be a consciously
willed one, since that would imply an objectified goal which the
experiencer brings to the experience.) Second, no-thought involves
one's full participation in the present. In the story, the second
monk's ability to respond spontaneously to a request for assistance
is contrasted sharply with the hesitant, passive, Hamlet-like cere-
bration of the first monk. No-thought or no-mind is not an unconscious state at all; it is an active, responsive awareness of the con-

tents of experience as directly experienced (before the intervention of complex intellectual activity).

The Zen doctrine of no-mind has much in common with the Taoist *wu-wei*. In both cases one achieves one's creative potential by eliminating egotistical considerations. In Taoism, we saw this idea expressed as the inner Nonbeing's becoming determinate through its interaction with Being. In Zen, one goes beyond emptiness as mere nondualism in order to bring it back into the world of form. As Zen Master Sasaki says:

> It is not Zen to have studied and to say, "I am empty. I am nothing." That's not Zen at all. You manifest yourself as emptiness or nothingness and you also have to manifest yourself as a man or a woman at the same time. At that moment you can say that you have mastered Zen.[13]

For both Zen and Taoism, nondualism is the *ground* of the everyday world. By returning to the indeterminate, one finds oneself again in the world of the determinate.

## HEIDEGGER'S *GELASSENHEIT:* A WESTERN PARALLEL TO NO-MIND?

This notion of no-mind seems rather exotic, but in Heidegger's description of meditative thinking, for example, there are striking parallels. In his *Discourse on Thinking*, Heidegger distinguishes calculative from meditative thinking: the former takes given conditions "into account with the calculated intent of their serving specific purposes," but the latter is content to "dwell on what lies close and meditate on what is closest; upon that which concerns us, each one of us, here and now" (pp. 46–47).[14]

In the second part of the *Discourse on Thinking*, Heidegger relates a discussion on *Gelassenheit* ("releasement" in the translation),* an apparent synonym for meditative thinking, especially insofar as it is opposed to *vorstellen* ("to re-present" in the English translation). Throughout this short conversation, we find several passages close in tone and significance to our discussion of no-

---

*The term *Gelassenheit* is difficult to translate in a single word. It refers, basically, to a state of composure arising out of an attitude of letting things be.

mind. Heidegger writes that *Gelassenheit* is (like no-mind) a "thinking that is not a willing" (pp. 59–60), "beyond the distinction
between activity and passivity" (p. 61). In very Taoist terms he
speaks of the "region" which "gathered just as if nothing were happening" (p. 66); everything there "returns to that in which it rests"
(p. 65). Associating *Gelassenheit* with "waiting," he says that "in
the region in which we stay everything is in the best order only if it
has been no one's doing" (p. 71). Along similar lines, the speakers
in the conversation repeatedly discover their inability to put into
words the phenomenon with which they are concerned (p. 75):

| | |
|---|---|
| Scholar: | Thus we are and we are not [truly appropriated to that-which-regions]. |
| Scientist: | Again this restless to and fro between yes and no. |
| Scholar: | We are suspended as it were between the two. |
| Teacher: | Yet our stand in this betweenness is waiting. |

Even the terms used by Heidegger's characters are reminiscent of
Mumon's "moment of yes-and-no." In fact, the reflections on *why*
this aspect of experience is ineffable are strikingly like the Zen
view; Heidegger's speakers find themselves trying to talk about the
"prior of everything" (p. 75):

| | |
|---|---|
| Scientist: | The prior of which we really cannot think . . . |
| Teacher: | . . . because the nature of thinking begins there. |

This is similar to the Chinese Taoist and Zen Buddhist concern for
the *source* of the distinction between Being and Nonbeing, yes and
no. Like Nāgārjuna, the speakers in the conversation are aware of
meditative thinking's resistance to making things into objects; they
are also alert to the danger of descriptions that reify (p. 67).
Similar to the Buddhist experience of *anātman* or "no-ego," the
characters in Heidegger's conversation see themselves becoming
more "waitful and void" and "apparently emptier, but richer in
contingencies" (p. 82). Contrasted with the subject–object distinctions made in calculative thought (p. 79), the "indwelling" in
meditative thinking is a "spontaneity of thinking" (p. 81)—again
terms reminiscent of the Zen doctrine of no-mind.

   In such a comparison, however, the differences are often as
revealing as the similarities. For example, Heidegger believes that

each kind of thinking, calculative and meditative, is "justified and needed in its own way" (p. 46) and that meditative thinking must be "pitted against" the post-Cartesian tendency toward the exclusive use of calculative thinking (p. 53). The Zen view of no-mind is at odds with both points. First, no-mind is more basic than, and even preliminary to, the scientific thinking which bifurcates subject and object. Therefore, from the Zen view, scientific and meditative thinking are *not* equally necessary or equally justifiable. No-mind involves a basic reorientation of consciousness; it is not merely a piece in the repertoire of consciousness. In other words, no-mind is characteristic of the state of permanent enlightenment; it is not a *kind* of thinking complementing other kinds of thinking. From this Zen perspective, Heidegger's meditative thinking is too passive insofar as it can only grasp ultimate ontological issues but cannot function practically in the daily affairs necessary to survival. Nan'yō, though, insists that no-mind is a functional mind.

With regard to the second point, Zen Buddhists would not agree with Heidegger's implication that the dominance of calculative thinking is the result of recent technological development. Rather, the tendency to restrict oneself to a bifurcated, intellectualized mode of consciousness is a fundamental characteristic of human experience in *any* time or place. It is a manifestation of the egocentric propensity to see oneself as an enduring entity, abiding in the world but essentially separate from it. This is a theme to which we will return.

We will have the opportunity to make further comparisons between Zen Buddhism and Heidegger, but here we need only note that the description used by Zen Masters in referring to the fundamental basis of consciousness is not unique. Even a Western phenomenologist like Heidegger may push ordinary semantics and syntax to their limits of signification in such discussions. This doctrine of no-mind is the endpoint of the Zen process: the purpose that is no-purpose. It cannot be pointed out or even explicitly sought since its basic function is clear only when one realizes that experience can be directly assimilated, and responded to, without resorting to conceptual frameworks and analysis. As Zen Buddhists enter deeper into the context of nothingness, they find it more and more difficult to locate themselves within a structure or framework. Unlike the secular contexts defining the former sense of personhood, the uniquely Zen context *takes away* specific regulations of responsibility, *dissolves* presupposed categories of personhood, and *removes* intellectualizations concerning who or what one is.

## THE TRUE PERSON OF NO STATUS

The Zen image of the person is perhaps best summed up by Rinzai (Ch: Lin-chi) in his doctrine of the "true person of no status" (Jp: *mui shinnin*). D. T. Suzuki argues that this concept of the person, permeating Rinzai's *Records*, is the main focus of Rinzai Zen.[15] In this regard the following story about Rinzai is particularly relevant:

> "In this clump of raw flesh [Rinzai said] there is a true person of no status continually entering and exiting your [sense organs]. Those of you who have not yet authenticated [this fact], look! Look!"
> Then a monk came forward and asked, "What [sort of thing] is this person of no status?"
> Coming down from his seat, taking hold of the monk, Rinzai exclaimed, "Speak! Speak!"
> [Hesitating] the monk deliberated.
> Rinzai released him, saying, "The true person of no status, what a dried-up shit-stick he is," and then returned to his chamber.[16]

Overly concerned with the phrase "true person of no status," the monk in the story was out of touch with his present experience and could not respond immediately to Rinzai's unexpected challenge. Ironically, if he had been more aware of his present experiential data, he could have responded to Rinzai's command, manifesting the answer to his own question ("What sort of thing is this person of no status?"). Explaining Rinzai's view, Suzuki writes: "In other words, the individual we think of as body, vision, and consciousness—of what constitutes existence and function—is what Rinzai calls the true person of no status."[17]

Along parallel lines, Zen Masters often urge their students to display the original face—that is, what they are before all conceptualizations and learned responses. It is said that Enō brought at least one of his students to enlightenment through the following koan:

> Not thinking of good, not thinking of evil, just this moment, what is your original face before your mother and father were born?[18]

Like Jōshū's "*Mu!*", this has become one of the most popular koans in Zen training.

In other words, both Rinzai and Enō want their disciples to be directly aware of the experiential process underlying any meaning a person might assume. Since the person acquires meaning from the context in which he or she functions, Zen Masters try to create a context of *mu* that eludes specific categorization or delimitation. That is, by establishing a context unlike all other contexts, the uniquely Zen meaning of the individual—the true person of no status, the original face—is manifest. To what is it made manifest? To the consciousness of the no-context, the consciousness of nothingness: *mushin*, "no-mind."

In Part I of this book we have examined the context within which the Zen Buddhist achieves personhood. To accomplish this, we have discussed *mu* in terms of emptiness in Nāgārjuna, Non-being in Taoism, and nothingness in Zen. Because of the unusual nature of this concept and because the idea is, in some ways, foreign to traditional Western thought, this detailed treatment introduced us to a different set of cultural assumptions and perhaps even, in Heidegger's phrase, to another kind of thinking. With our new understanding of *mu* as a backdrop, Part II examines more closely the structure of Zen itself, particularly as a process of self-realization. We have circumambulated the Zen conception of *mu* long enough. It is now time to enter the consciousness it establishes and to continue our investigation within it:

> *Furuike ya*             Ah, the ancient pond.
> *Kawazu tobikomu*        A frog makes the plunge;
> *Mizu no oto.*[19]       The sound of water.
> —Bashō

# Part II
PERSONAL MEANING IN ZEN
PRACTICE

# CHAPTER 5

# Zen and Reality

In Part I, we investigated Zen's mistrust of conceptual distinctions and its belief that one should return to the immediate source of one's direct experience. Although we have used negative terms such as nothingness or no-mind, we have described Zen mostly in a positive sense up to now; we have emphasized what it maintains, not what it rejects. Yet the Zen quest, like most religious quests, begins with a spiritual discontent with ordinary existence. The first Noble Truth formally accepted by all Buddhists is the presence of suffering. The Sanskrit word for suffering *(duḥkha)* has many connotations, one of the key ones being *inadequacy.*

## ZEN'S REJECTION OF CONCEPTUAL CATEGORIES

The Zen Buddhist view is that intellectualizations, concepts, even language itself are inadequate for expressing our experience *as it is experienced.* We go through life thinking that our words and ideas mirror what we experience, but repeatedly we discover that the distinctions taken to be true are merely mental constructs. In verbalizing something, we may have a lingering sense of having compromised part of our experience, but we continue to devise new categories, new names for new things, more distinctions when a moment before there were no distinctions. When we first learned the word *philodendron,* for example, we gained a new communication skill: we could call a florist on the phone, order a philodendron, and expect a delivery meeting our specifications. From the Zen perspective, however, a subtle price is paid for this new facility

—namely, the *uniqueness* of each philodendron plant. Indeed, the uniqueness of each of our experiences of the same philodendron (as we walk around it or water it through the years) is pushed into the background. The word *philodendron* becomes a filter on our experience, a filter blurring the outlines of each member of the class *philodendron* so that we can focus on the class as a whole.

Thus, the conceptual filter, like any filter useful for some special effect, *distorts* the original image. Feeling an occasional sense of loss, we might try to compensate for it by expressing the inadequacy we feel. One might say, "Yes, but I also know that every philodendron is unique; each one is, in some discernible way, different from all the rest." Yet if one is fully honest with oneself, one recognizes something hollow in this attempt. If the word *philodendron* no longer rings true, can the words *unique* or *different* be any truer? It is as if we were continually adding new colored filters to compensate for the old ones, thereby trying to get a distortionless, colorless combination. The result, however, is only a further darkening of the image and an increase in our discontent. Frustrated, one might begin to question who or what one is. What is the relationship between one's name and the being that one is? One may laugh cynically at even this self-deception. The being that one is—what is this word *being?* One cannot even find a standpoint allowing one to pose the question, not to mention the answer.

## THE RETROSPECTIVE RECONSTRUCTION OF REALITY

In so questioning, we are ready for the Zen Master's demand to show our original face before our parents were born. There is nothing *new* to be learned, no new distinction-making filter that will clarify, no salvation outside ourselves. The Zen Master simply advises us to *return:* to go back to the state before we put on the first filter. But what is the master telling us to become? An infant-like preverbal consciousness that, making no distinctions, is incapable of communication? Certainly not. That would be an autistic route, a withdrawal from the world through the exclusion of all involvement with our own perceptions. Rather, we must

return to where we *are*. We must regain our grasp of the present
moment as it is being experienced.

This phrase "as it is being experienced" has occurred repeatedly
in our discussion, but we have not yet fully clarified its meaning.
Recall the story of the two monks and the maiden at the ford of the
river. Totally concerned with monastic rules (learned in the past)
and the consequences (in the future) of his actions, the first monk
was unable to respond to a present need. Certainly, this is a case of
not being able to relate to a situation as it is being experienced. But
our phrase means more than just being responsive to present situations. Certain learned categories are so much a part of our thinking
that we often forget they are filters blurring aspects of experience
in order to bring about some special effect or to highlight one facet
of a many-sided entity. We have noted, for example, that the state
of no-mind is supposed to be outside the bifurcation into subject
and object. To the Western philosopher who thinks of the subject/
object distinction as a priori, the Zen characterization is either
suspect or, at best, metaphorical. In any experience, the Westerner
might claim, we can distinguish the activity of an intentional consciousness and the content toward which that consciousness is
directed.

The Zen Buddhist, however, would emphasize the *time* at which
the distinction can be made: although we can retrospectively look
at a previous experience, analyzing its subject and object, that
experience, while it was being lived, was not so divided. While it is
correct in a certain sense to say that "I hit the baseball," for instance, this expression, with its division into subject and object, is
the result of a retrospective analysis. At the moment of the original
event, there is only an unbroken hitting-of-the-baseball. In fact, as
anyone who plays the game knows well enough, the thought of *I* as
something that must *hit* the *baseball* is an obstruction to hitting the
ball well. Having developed the technical mastery of the swing, the
batter best performs by *not* thinking about hitting—that is, not by
reflecting on what was learned or on what must be done, but
rather by simply being alert. Then, at the moment when the ball is
to be hit, one can react spontaneously.

This analogy from baseball introduces a distinction helpful in our investigation of what Zen Buddhism is reacting against in ordinary experience. We can consider two different modes of behavior: one exemplified by the novice player still learning the rules and techniques of the game and the other exemplified by the skillful player who purely responds to the ball's coming over the plate, with no thought of I or ball. Although the novice is always thinking about what he or she is doing while doing it (left shoulder down, eye on the ball, shifting weight to the front leg), the accomplished player, once readied in the batter's box, ceases such dualistic thoughts and becomes purely reactive. Hinging total awareness on the pivotal moment we call the present, he or she merely waits, poised to respond to the virtually infinite number of paths the ball might travel.

The Zen Buddhist critique of unenlightened life is that we resemble the novice. We accept various distinctions and conceptual characterizations of reality, allowing them to interfere with our ability to be spontaneous and grounded in the present. We classify persons into various categories (man/woman, white/black, I/you), for example, letting them obstruct our direct relationship with others. As Western consciousness has become aware of the distortions inherent in these classifications, it has designated new categories to replace the old ones (women's liberation, racial equality, the I-Thou relationship). Yet one can easily become as attached to these categories as to the previous ones—and the same obstructions to directness ensue. A similar phenomenon occurs in our relationship to the natural world. For centuries the West viewed nature through one set of categories (natural resources, energy, an object for human use) but, aware of the inadequacy of those categories, has now established new ones (organic food, pollution factors, ecology). The Zen Buddhists claim, though, that as long as we see any set of categories as the *right* ones, we will inevitably fall back into that same feeling of dissatisfaction. Nature will always remain a *thing*, and the current characterization of it will interfere with our ability to experience nature directly.[1]

The goal of Zen training is to break down our dependence on categories that interfere with the directness and immediacy of experience, but this does not mean that thought stops altogether. In the

preceding chapter, we saw Nan'yō insist that no-mind *(wu-hsin)* is
not separate from functional mind *(yung-hsin)*. Returning to the
analogy of the accomplished baseball player, there is, first of all,
something naive in the major leaguer. Without thinking about I
and ball, he is akin to a boy who unselfconsciously picks up a stick
and swats at a leaf falling from a tree. From this perspective, the
professional returns to a primordial state of consciousness. In one
sense, his goal is to regain that childlike immediacy. Yet, in
another sense, he is different from the youngster. No child could
stroll into Yankee Stadium and hit the ball out of the park. The
accomplished major leaguer has to undergo a strenuous and
detailed schedule of training (what Zen calls the "discipline"—
*shugyō*). Why is this necessary? Though the boy was like the professional in his immediacy, he was not like him in proficiency. The
boy would have no chance against a bulletlike slider thrown by a
major league pitcher. First he must learn the proper techniques of
batting. The immediacy cannot be taught, but the proficiency must
be practiced. After a sufficiently long period of training, the proper
technique of the swing becomes second nature and the player no
longer thinks about what he is doing while doing it. He begins to
hit the ball better than ever.

Like the baseball player, the Zen monk is interested in preserving
immediacy, but the myriad forms of life situations present a baf-
fling assortment of possibilities to which one must respond. As with
the novice in Yankee Stadium a childlike innocence is no asset: the
monk must, to a certain extent, *learn* how to respond. Ideas, words,
and categories all have their place, but the Zen Buddhist, unlike
other people, is trained to be explicitly aware of the limitations of
concepts. The Zen monk recognizes that no new "-ism," not even
Zen Buddhism, will be satisfactory. Knowing that one must leave
behind all doctrines, even those of Zen Buddhism, the novice aban-
dons himself or herself to *mu*. In this way, Zen supersedes other
forms of training. The Zen Buddhist must have insight not only
into a single discipline (as the baseball player knows why the
shoulder must be kept down and also why one must not think
about keeping it down while swinging), but also into the very
nature of discipline itself. Developing an insight into one's own pro-

cesses of consciousness, the Zen Buddhist must learn to recognize presuppositions inhibiting one's ability to relate in the present, master a method for eliminating the dependence on such presuppositions, and discard whatever concepts or categories were used in destroying that dependence on presuppositions.

It is evident, then, that thought is understood to be an *intermediary* stage. When immediacy is blocked by some new phenomenon or by some previously unnoticed presupposition, one may think in order to eliminate the obstruction, but one does so only until one can again abandon reflective conceptualization and return to immediacy. Analogously, when a major leaguer goes into a slump, the batting coach may suggest a change in the player's technique, perhaps a different stance. As soon as the new stance feels natural, however, the player no longer thinks about it—he again returns to his immediacy. The primary difference between Zen training and sports training is scope. While baseball is limited to the experience of hitting, throwing, and catching a ball, Zen Buddhism attempts to train the monk for *any* experience. To achieve this unlimited scope, the Zen Master must train the disciple to penetrate the processes of consciousness itself, rather than the specifics of any single manifestation.

In summation, Zen Buddhism criticizes our ordinary, unenlightened existence by refusing to accept a retrospective reconstruction of reality. Ordinary experience is *retrospective* in that we try to understand experience through previously learned categories. By allowing these categories to color our present experience and restrict our immediacy, we determine our everyday experience by distinctions such as student/teacher, man/woman, white/black, natural resources/organic food. Our common understanding of experience is therefore a *reconstruction* in that it imposes categories that were not present in that experience when it originally occurred. Thus, although one properly says retrospectively "I hit the ball," it does not follow that when the actual hitting took place, there was a consciousness of I and ball as separate entities. In reconstructing a past experience, we isolate aspects of the experience that were not isolated within the original experience as it occurred.

Lastly, ordinary experience has a sense of *reality* quite at odds with Zen. For the unenlightened, reality is what exists outside our experience; it is the object or content of experience. But Zen Buddhism, like John Dewey, rejects any such notion of the "antecedently real." Dewey claims that philosophers have traditionally thought their object of investigation to be "a higher realm of fixed reality" and that "the office of knowledge is to uncover the antecedently real, rather than, as in the case with our practical judgments, to gain the kind of understanding which is necessary to deal with problems as they arise."[2]

Zen Buddhism and Dewey agree that reality is what is now happening—it is not outside our experience, but the construct being worked out in our experience. For Zen, this has the implication that reality is protean, always changing its shape as soon as we come into contact with it and try to pin it down. By living in the present moment, there is no longer the tendency to make reality into something static or reified.

## EXPERIENCE AND THE ANALYTIC MODE: TWO CRITICISMS

This retrospective reconstruction of reality, then, is the core of the inadequacy of unenlightened existence, the heart of the discontent initiating an interest in the Zen way of life. But *why* is Zen's emphasis on immediacy preferable to this analytic mode of consciousness? Can Zen Buddhists *argue* their position? There are two lines to offer in Zen's defense.

First, following Nāgārjuna's dialectical disputation, we could argue that the distinctions on which analysis depends are intrinsically self-destructive. Thus, every (re-)construction of reality necessarily encapsulates irresolvable oppositions.[3] To use language without being trapped by it, one's understanding of reality must be based in the immediate, nonverbal intuition of *prajñā*. Then, if one finds it necessary to describe or analyze phenomena, one will be cognizant of which aspects of the primordial experience are being highlighted and which hidden by the distinctions. By recognizing the limitations of language and conceptualization, one can use them without being misled by them.

The second argument offered in Zen's defense is that of NISHIDA

Kitarō, a twentieth-century Japanese philosopher. In his first major work, A *Study of Good*, he developed his concept of "pure experience" *(junsui keiken)*, an idea loosely derived from his reading of William James and from his own experiences in a Zen monastery. In the opening pages of the book, Nishida characterizes pure experience as a mental activity devoid of the bifurcations into subject and object as well as of "the least thought or reflection"; that is, objects are experienced "without attaching any meaning to them at all."[4] From this perspective, pure experience is a nonreflective form of consciousness, its key characteristics being spontaneity, unity, and presentness.[5] Nishida offers two examples: a musician's experience of playing a piece he knows well and Goethe's of composing a poem during a dream.

This characterization of pure experience seems clear enough: Nishida obviously has in mind some form of intuitive, nondiscursive consciousness. But in continuing his account, he seems to equivocate, saying that *all* forms of consciousness are really pure experience: "But seen from the standpoint of the theory of pure experience, we are unable ever to go outside of the scope of pure experience."[6]

How can Nishida say this? If pure experience lacks the least thought or reflection, how can all experiences be pure? According to Nishida, thoughts, judgments, and categories arise only when there is some *break* in the unified field of pure experience. This contention is reminiscent of the pragmatists' claim that thought arises only in response to something problematical. At that moment of disunity, Nishida argues, nothing is more directly experienced than that disunity itself. Hence, even thought is a kind of pure experience insofar as it is an immediate, unwilled response to what is directly given in experience. In this line of argument, thought is not essentially distinguishable in its operation from supposedly pure experiences such as direct perception (although the nature of the object of thought might differ somewhat from that of the object of perception):

Usually it is held that perceptual experience is passive and its activity is all unconscious whereas thought, on the contrary, is active and all its activity is conscious. But where is there such a clear distinction? Even thought, when it operates and develops freely, takes place under an almost unconscious attention, and its becoming conscious means, on the contrary, that this advance is impeded. That which causes thought to progress is not our voluntary activity; thought advances of itself. When we wholly cast away our ego and become one with the object of our thought, namely our problem, . . . we first see the operation of thought. . . . Perhaps we are able to say that the merging with our object, i.e., the turning of our attention, is voluntary, but on this point I think that perception is the same; for we are able freely to turn our attention and see those objects which we wish to see. . . . Thought, too, when one shifts from one representation to another, is unconscious and while the unifying process is operating in reality, it must be unconscious. When one is conscious of a thing as an object, already that activity belongs to the past.[7]

In short, pure experience is unavoidable because present experience is unavoidable. Whatever the object of an experience may be, whether a physical thing, memory, or concept, that experience occurs in the present. As Sartre has pointed out in his *Transcendence of the Ego*, even when we are self-conscious, the *agent* of that self-consciousness is not reflected upon.[8] There must always remain the unselfconscious entity having the self-consciousness; any attempt to capture the self is directed toward the self that *was*, not the self that is.

In summing up these points Nishida writes: "Thus an event of pure experience is the alpha of thought and its omega as well. In fine, thought is nothing more than a process in the development of and realization of a great system of consciousness."[9] In other words, thought emerges out of pure experience insofar as it is an immediate, unselfconsciously willed response to a problematic situation arising within pure experience. Furthermore, once its task has been completed and the problematic has been interpreted and reintegrated into a unified consciousness, pure experience without thought again reigns. Therefore, like our previous discussion of no-mind, Nishida's account of pure experience regards thought as a necessary—but intermediary—moment in the development of unbifurcated consciousness.

This, then, is our second critique of the strictly analytic view of consciousness. If one takes the analytic mode to be the essence of consciousness, immediacy cannot be integrated into the system and must be viewed as a disruption or suspension of reflective consciousness.[10] On the other hand, the immediacy advocated by the Zen Buddhist, here represented by Nishida, is more inclusive than the analytic view in that it can account for the experience of both analysis and immediacy within *one* description of consciousness. Nishida's view describes thought itself as an immediate as well as a necessary moment in the systematic continuity of unified consciousness. Not only does Nishida wish to include in his explication *only* what is experienced; he also wants to include *everything* so experienced. It is on this point that Nishida is closest to William James's radical empiricism: "To be radical, an empiricism must neither admit into its constructions any element that is not directly experienced, nor exclude from them any element that is directly experienced."[11] On these grounds he would criticize a strictly analytic view of consciousness as being not inclusive enough.

In summation, then, Zen reacts against what we have called the retrospective reconstruction of reality, the source of the inadequacy of unenlightened existence. From the Zen Buddhist view of consciousness, thought is effective only when it arises spontaneously out of a problematic situation. Whenever the person willfully thinks, whenever one tries to make experience fit retrospectively derived categories, that thinking inevitably leads to paradoxes and conflicts. When thought arises as a spontaneous response to a break in immediacy, however, it serves as an intermediary stage in the return to spontaneity.

This chapter has focused on the way ordinary experience falls short of expectations and leaves us with a need that the Zen way of life tries to meet. But how exactly does Zen practice address these concerns? How does the Zen Buddhist achieve immediacy? How is it disrupted? How can thought arise *spontaneously?* To answer these questions, we will enlist the help of Dōgen in the next two chapters. Dōgen's writings are not easy: he challenges our intellectual resources in a way that only a combined Zen Master–philosopher can.

# CHAPTER 6

# Dōgen's Phenomenology of Zazen

In this chapter and the next we will discuss the central practice of
Zen Buddhism—namely, Zen meditation or zazen—making particular reference to the writings of Zen Master DŌGEN Kigen
(1200–1253). The purpose of this investigation is twofold. First,
insofar as zazen is a state of consciousness (or produces a state of
consciousness) verifying the Zen standpoint, a phenomenology of
what it is and how it functions is particularly relevant. Second, as
one of Zen's most philosophical masters, Dōgen tries to articulate
the relationships between thought and satori and between Zen practice and Zen philosophy. This chapter ties together some loose ends
in our philosophical analysis and takes us directly into the very
heart of Zen practice, thereby clarifying the Zen alternative to the
retrospective reconstruction of reality.

Born in 1200, Dōgen was one of the key figures in the Kamakura period's revitalization of Buddhism in Japan. Previously,
Japanese Buddhism tended to emphasize the analysis of complex
metaphysical theories and the performance of esoteric rituals, thus
serving best the more aristocratic echelons of society—those who
could read Chinese as well as Japanese and who had the time to
study the intricacies of Buddhist doctrines and rituals. During the
Kamakura period (1185–1333), new Buddhist schools developed in
Japan including various Zen, Pure Land, and Nichiren orders.
These "new" schools (most had either direct or indirect roots in
China) stressed practical disciplines to be undertaken by religious
and lay people alike, thus opening up the benefits of Buddhism to
all. Dōgen, inadvertently at first, found himself part of this movement.

Of aristocratic background, Dōgen was traditionally trained in the literary arts, having been introduced to Chinese poetry, for example, at the age of four. He lost both parents by the age of seven. Tradition suggests that this experience sensitized him to the transience of life and motivated him to pursue enlightenment.[1] Refusing an opportunity to become the heir of an aristocratic uncle, Dōgen fled home and was eventually ordained a monk at Mt. Hiei in Kyoto, the center of the Tendai branch of Buddhism in Japan and one of the most influential temples in the country at the time. His quick mind and studious attitude helped him to grasp many of the complex metaphysical analyses and esoteric rituals of the Tendai order, but he became preoccupied with a nagging question about Buddhist teaching:

> As I study both the exoteric and the esoteric schools of Buddhism, they maintain that man is endowed with the Dharma-nature by birth. If this is the case, why had the Buddhas of all ages—undoubtedly in possession of enlightenment—to seek enlightenment and engage in spiritual practice?[2]

In other words, if in some sense we are already enlightened, if all beings are already Buddha, why is enlightenment so difficult to achieve? Why, in effect, must one undergo any religious discipline at all? This question had special meaning for Dōgen since Tendai itself seemed ambivalent at the time. On the one hand, doctrinal studies emphasized "primordial enlightenment" *(hongaku)*; but, on the other, the practical training seemed to stress "acquired enlightenment" *(shikaku)*, the result of years of disciplined practice.

To find the answer to his question, Dōgen undertook a spiritual quest, wandering from teacher to teacher. Together with Myōzen, the abbot of a newly established Rinzai Zen temple in Kyoto, Kennin-ji, Dōgen traveled to China in 1223 to seek the roots of Zen and the resolution of his problem. After two years, he met the famous Chinese Zen Master Nyōjo (Ch: Ju-ching; 1163–1228) and enthusiastically became his disciple. A zealously strict disciplinarian, Nyōjo urged his students to practice zazen virtually day and night. One day, the monk seated next to Dōgen fell asleep during evening meditation and the master exclaimed, "In Zen, body and mind are molted. Why do you sleep?" Hearing these words, Dōgen was suddenly enlightened. After being certified by the master,

Dōgen remained in China two more years and in 1227 returned to Japan, claiming to have brought back with him none of the customary images or scriptures, but only the clarity of his realization and his intent to preach the prodigious value of zazen. Although he clearly stated repeatedly that he did not seek to establish a sect or school of Buddhism called "Zen," Dōgen is traditionally considered to be the founder of Japanese Sōtō Zen.

## DŌGEN'S PHILOSOPHICAL PROJECT

How, then, did Dōgen answer his original question? From his new standpoint, he saw that the initial issue posed on Mt. Hiei had falsely separated practice from realization, cultivation *(shu)* from authentication *(shō)*. That is, meditation had been taken to be a *means* to an end, a technique by which one might achieve enlightenment or satori. This distinction between methods and goals, Dōgen came to believe, was erroneous: zazen is not a technique by which to achieve enlightenment; it is enlightenment itself. Consequently, the hallmark of Dōgen's Zen is *shikantaza*—"nothing but sitting" or, more simply, "just sitting." Upon returning to Japan, Dōgen's first written work was, naturally enough, a brief description of the method of sitting in zazen. Written in Japanized Chinese *(kambun)*, it was simply called *Fukanzazengi* [Universal promotion of the principles of zazen]. In a moment, we will turn to this document.

Because of the turmoil taking place within Japanese Buddhism at the time, it was soon evident that merely describing zazen would not be enough. Dōgen had to justify it to those skeptics who either denied its primacy or accepted it only as a means to a goal but not as an equivalent to realization itself. In response, Dōgen recorded his lectures and compiled his essays into a collection known as *Shōbōgenzō* [Treasury of the correct dharma-eye].* Unlike earlier

---

*The word *dharma* (Jp: *HŌ, nori*) has no single English equivalent. Its range of meanings include: (1) (moral) law; (2) teaching or doctrine (by extension, the Buddhist doctrine, that is, Truth); (3) causal condition; (4) thing or atom; (5) phenomenon. Since Dōgen uses the term in several senses, only context can distinguish which meaning is appropriate in a given case, but he most often uses *dharma* to mean either doctrine (True Doctrine) or things as experienced. The "correct dharma-eye," therefore, indicates the enlightened viewpoint.

Japanese Buddhist commentaries, *Shōbōgenzō* was written in Japanese rather than Chinese. In fact, it was the first comprehensive philosophical work to be written in Japanese. Even today, many scholars consider this rich compilation of the master's teachings to be the most sophisticated treatise in Japanese religious thought. Before actually investigating excerpts, let us make some observations about its general nature.

The complexity of *Shōbōgenzō* lies partly in its creative style. Pushing the medieval Japanese language to its expressive limits, Dōgen interweaves the idiomatic and the traditional: even the most complex and convoluted discussions are interlaced with strikingly concrete and poetic images. Dōgen often writes statements having at least two levels of meaning, and he is particularly skillful in using traditional Buddhist terms to function simultaneously as naturalistic images and descriptions of states of mind. In English, for example, we can speak of foggy minds as well as foggy weather. Dōgen uses such wordplay in Japanese to give, simultaneously, a concrete description of a natural event as well as a phenomenological description of a state of mind. He also freely devises new words when it suits his purpose. Together, these elements make *Shōbōgenzō* not only philosophically provoking but also poetic. Above all, however, it is idiosyncratic and difficult to interpret conclusively.

Perhaps most striking is Dōgen's radical reinterpretation of classical Chinese Buddhist passages. Like most contributors to the development of Buddhism, Dōgen considers his teaching to be strictly traditional; that is, he believes *Shōbōgenzō* to be a compendium of the "correct Dharma" *(shōbō)*, a rediscovery of Buddhism's essence. To support the claim that he is a traditionalist, Dōgen often quotes classical scriptures, but in doing so he often gives the Chinese phrases creative, and very unorthodox, readings. For example, he interprets the phrase *uji* (which usually means "at a certain time" or "when") as "being-time." Although this interpretation is eccentric, technically speaking, the characters do lend themselves to such a meaning.[3] Similarly, a Chinese line meaning "all [sentient] beings have Buddha-nature" *(issai shujō shitsu u busshō)* is transformed into "all is sentient being; all beings are Buddha-nature";[4] "do no evil" (shoakumakusa) becomes "[the state of] the nonproduction of evil."[5] Dōgen's sensitivity to the possibilities and nuances of language goes beyond mere stylistics, though. To understand the real meaning of such key Buddhist phrases, he maintains, requires nothing less than penetrating the core of Buddhism itself.

Before discussing Dōgen's ideas per se, however, one further point about his general philosophical perspective should be raised, especially since it is often overlooked and can be the source of great confusion. As noted already, Dōgen felt obliged to justify his advocacy of zazen. To do so involved a rigorous investigation into the nature of zazen itself. It is critical, though, that Dōgen came to believe that the mode of consciousness in zazen is fundamental in all modes of consciousness. That is, to understand zazen is to understand consciousness in general. In this way, Dōgen becomes fundamentally *phenomenological* in perspective.* Rather than trying to develop an epistemological or metaphysical system, Dōgen's

---

*This term *phenomenological* should not be taken in too strict a Husserlian sense, however. Dōgen has no clear position vis-à-vis intentionality, but he does subscribe to a primitive gestalt theory in that he believes one's situational context and past conditioning affect the way one perceives phenomena. To this extent, Dōgen is aware of the function of intentionality even though he has no developed theory of it. As for another mainstay of phenomenology—bracketing—Dōgen has a clearer stance.

In Husserl's terminology, bracketing means to suspend all presuppositions as to what causes one to have a certain experience. One accepts the experience in its own terms without assuming or denying that there is a world independent of one's experience. We must bear in mind that Dōgen comes at the end of a long evolution of Buddhist philosophy, beginning with an empirical emphasis in Early Buddhism, proceeding through metaphysical speculation (Abhidharma Buddhism), epistemological skepticism (Mādhyamika Buddhism), and idealism (Yogācāra Buddhism). The culmination is in the totalistic monisms of Hua-yen and T'ien-t'ai and the esotericism of the *mikkyō* tradition in Japan. Thus, Dōgen is not a naive realist insofar as he is sensitive to the contribution of mind in the constituting of experience. Yet he is no subjective idealist either. Although mind cannot be separated from reality, reality cannot thereby be reduced to mind. Dōgen's tack is to concern himself only with what is experienced. Limiting himself to this, he is not concerned with notions of reality outside this process of experiencing consciousness. In *Shōbōgenzō*, Dōgen frequently takes a seemingly metaphysical statement from the T'ien-t'ai or Hua-yen traditions and interprets it as a descriptive statement about the structure of a specific experience; in effect, he suspends metaphysical and epistemological commitments outside the realm of things as experienced. In this respect, Dōgen is implicitly carrying out his own form of bracketing and the term *phenomenological* is surprisingly appropriate to characterize the nature of his methodology.

main philosophical concern is to characterize the nature of human experience, especially in its preconceptual or prereflective dimension. In the experience of zazen, the phenomenological difference between the prereflective and reflective is most evident and, therefore, his consideration of zazen deals not only with the psychospiritual aspects of this religious practice, but also implies certain philosophical conclusions about the nature of consciousness at large. In Dōgen more than in any other Zen Master, there is a comprehensive attempt at explicating the nature of the Zen experience and showing its relationship to ordinary, unenlightened consciousness.

## DŌGEN'S ACCOUNT OF ZAZEN

In order to understand Dōgen's philosophical analysis, it is important to have a clear idea of how zazen is practiced. The term *zazen* literally means "seated meditation." The term *zen* is ultimately derived from the Sanskrit word *dhyāna*, a general term referring to various meditative disciplines and their accompanying states of consciousness. Hence, Zen Buddhism stresses *dhyāna* or meditation. All Buddhists are supposed to meditate, of course, but the practice varies among schools. For a description of Japanese Zen Buddhist meditation, no one is more explicit than Dōgen. Let us begin with his first major writing, the previously mentioned *Fukanzazengi*. Dōgen was apparently quite satisfied with this description, since he rewrote it into Japanese with only slight revisions as a chapter in *Shōbōgenzō*, where it is simply called "Zazengi" [Principles of zazen]. Although the technique of seated meditation had been known for centuries in Japan, Dōgen helped to revitalize its practice. His description became paradigmatic:

> For *sanzen* [in this case, doing zazen as instructed by a master], a quiet room is suitable. Eat and drink moderately. Cast aside all involvements and cease all affairs. Do not think good or bad. Do not administer pros and cons. Cease all movements of the conscious mind, the gauging of all thoughts and views. Have no designs on becoming a Buddha. *(Sanzen)* has nothing whatever to do with sitting or lying down.

At the site of your regular sitting, spread out thick matting and place a cushion above it. Sit either in the full-lotus or half-lotus position. . . . Then place your right hand on your left leg and your left palm (facing upwards) on your right palm, thumb-tips touching. Thus sit upright in correct bodily posture, neither inclining to the left nor to the right, neither leaning forward or backward. Be sure your eyes are on a plane with your shoulders and your nose in line with your navel. Place your tongue against the front roof of your mouth, with teeth and lips both shut. Your eyes should always remain open, and you should breathe gently through your nose.

Once you have adjusted your posture, take a deep breath, inhale and exhale, rock your body right and left and settle into a steady, immobile sitting position. Think of not thinking. How do you think of not-thinking? Without thinking. This in itself is the essential art of zazen.

The zazen I speak of is not learning meditation. It is simply the Dharma-gate of repose and bliss, the cultivation-authentication of totally culminated enlightenment. It is the presence of things as they are.[6]

As simple as this passage might seem, there are nonetheless phrases requiring further elaboration. What does Dōgen mean by the set of terms "thinking" (shiryō), "not-thinking" (fushiryō), and "without-thinking" (hishiryō)?[7] What is the significance of the phrase "cultivation-authentication" (shushō)? And what is the "presence of things as they are" (kōan genjō)? To understand these terms is to enter into the heart of Dōgen's thought.

## THINKING, NOT-THINKING, WITHOUT-THINKING

These three terms—thinking, not-thinking, without-thinking—are not of Dōgen's invention. There is a traditional mondō (Zen dialogue) utilizing the same distinctions, and Dōgen quotes it in the opening of his Shōbōgenzō fascicle "Zazenshin" [Counsel about zazen]:

Once, after Master YAKUSAN Gudō [Ch: YÜEH-SHAN Hung-tao (745–828)] was sitting [in zazen], a monk asked him, "When you are sitting immovably, about what do you think?" The Master replied, "I think about not thinking [about anything]." The monk responded, "How does one think about not-thinking?" The Master replied, "Without thinking."[8]

Modern commentators on Dōgen have discussed the threefold distinction in a way directly relevant to our previous discussions. In a brief note, TAKAHASHI Masanobu takes the following line. *Shiryō* (what we are calling "thinking") is "considering with the intent of weighing ideas." *Fushiryō* ("not-thinking") in its "absolute" sense (that is, in its technical usage here) is simply the negation or denial of *shiryō*. *Hishiryō* ("without-thinking"), however, goes "beyond thinking and not-thinking."[9] Takahashi's point is that one may affirm (through thinking) or negate (through not-thinking) the value or relevance of the products of ideation. Yet, as the third term, without-thinking, implies, there is another standpoint one might take: merely accepting the presence of ideation without either affirmation or denial. Let us look at this third term more closely.

Terada and Mizuno in their edition of *Dōgen* regard the difference between not-thinking and without-thinking as the difference between a simple negation and the Buddhist doctrine of emptiness *(kū; Skrt: śūnyatā):*

> Without-thinking is emptiness. Not-thinking is the denial of thinking. In that *kū* transcends the distinction between subject and object and being and nothingness, to say that without-thinking is "crystal clear" [as Dōgen does in "Zazenshin"] is justified.[10]

To relate without-thinking to the notion of nothingness recalls our earlier discussion of no-mind. Yet, in implying a special relationship with thinking, Dōgen's term is more specific than the general notion of no-mind. Another Japanese commentator on Dōgen, AKIYAMA Hanji, describes this relationship in more detail:

> Among the three [terms] there is discerned to be a dialectical relationship. Thinking is all of the acts of consciousness—perceptual experience, judgmental thought, carnal desires, delusions, etc.—a general term for all of the situations of knowledge, emotion, or will.[11]

As for not-thinking: "when read as 'to not think,' it is understood as the denial of 'thinking,' as the cutting off of consciousness and nihilation *(kūmu)*."[12]

As Akiyama himself perceives, this form of denial is problematic. From what standpoint, we might ask, can we speak of the denial of thought? Is not that denial itself a thought? "For not-thinking as the denial of thinking means the annihilation of consciousness, but this annihilation of consciousness, is itself impossible."[13] We need a third standpoint, one that would allow us to make not-thinking conscious but would not itself be included in the category of thinking. In other words, without-thinking allows us to recognize not-thinking as itself a thought (thereby revealing it to be a thought which denies thought). This implies that without-thinking is a more basic mode of consciousness than either thinking or not-thinking, and Akiyama is led to speak of a *dialectical* relationship: "In other words, without-thinking sublates thinking and not-thinking and is that which unifies them."[14] On these grounds, without-thinking is not a negation without content. Indeed, it affirms the very relationship between thinking and not-thinking, and Akiyama asserts, "Both thinking and not-thinking are without-thinking."[15]

The relationships among these three terms may be further clarified by assuming, as suggested earlier, a more formally phenomenological perspective. Specifically, we may analyze their noetic and noematic aspects.[16] First let us try to formalize the relationships by the following scheme:

1.  Thinking ·
    noetic attitude: positional (either affirming or negating)
    noematic content: conceptualized objects
2.  Not-thinking
    noetic attitude: positional (only negating)
    noematic content: thinking (as objectified)
3.  Without-thinking
    noetic attitude: nonpositional (neither affirming nor negating)
    noematic content: pure presence of things as they are

To elucidate these technical terms, we will now consider examples of each of the three modes: thinking, not-thinking, and without-thinking.

*Thinking* includes most of what we typically regard as consciousness—that is, any mental act whereby we explicitly or implicitly take a stance toward some object, whether that stance be emotional, judgmental, believing, remembering, or assumptive. Whether I judge the lamp to be or not to be on the table, whether I believe or do not believe it to be a lamp, whether I remember or forget the lamp's color, whether I try to turn it on or bump into it (on the assumption that it is or is not in a given place)—insofar as all these mental attitudes take a position with regard to an object (the lamp or the concept of the lamp), they are all examples of thinking *(shiryō)*.

*Not-thinking,* in its intentional or *act* aspect, is like certain forms of thinking in that it takes a negating, denying, or rejecting attitude. It is distinguished from thinking only in its noematic aspect —that is, only with regard to the *what* toward which it takes its position. The object of not-thinking's intentionality is thinking *(shiryō)* itself. In other words, not-thinking is essentially a negating attitude toward all the mental acts indicated in the preceding paragraph. Although the terminology makes this mode of consciousness seem exotic, it is really commonplace. Thinking and worrying about some personal problems, for example, a man cannot fall asleep. Finally, he resolves to stop thinking about everything and get some rest. Rolling over, he takes a deep breath and makes a conscious effort to blank his mind and break off all trains of thought. Clearly, this effort qualifies as a genuine mental act: there is not only an intentional attitude but also an object of intentionality. The man's will is directed toward something specific, but that something is not a simple object or concept (as in thinking). It is the process of conceptualization itself. This is what is meant by not-thinking *(fushiryō)*.

A prevalent misconception about Zen meditation is that it is a form of not-thinking. Dōgen clearly rejects this view; that is, zazen is *not* a conscious effort to blank one's mind or turn off all conceptual processes. As Master Uchiyama observed (Chapter 4), although one should sit in zazen as immovably as a rock, one should not try to be as unconscious as a rock. To achieve such a state is not only not zazen, it is also impossible. So Dōgen maintains that zazen is better characterized by without-thinking *(hishiryō)*.

*Without-thinking* is distinct from thinking and not-thinking precisely in its assuming *no* intentional attitude whatsoever: it neither affirms nor denies, accepts nor rejects, believes nor disbelieves. In fact, it does not objectify either implicitly or explicitly. In this respect, the noetic (or act aspect) of without-thinking is completely different from that of thinking or not-thinking. Even though without-thinking circumvents all objectification, it is nonetheless a mode of consciousness, and through reflection on a without-thinking act, one may isolate aspects of its formal contents. The point, though, is that at the time of without-thinking's actual occurrence, those contents were neither affirmed nor negated—they were merely an unobjectified presence without any conscious or unconscious attitude directed toward them. In short, it is a non-conceptual or prereflective mode of consciousness.[17] Let us consider an example.

In ordinary life, prereflective experiences are often only fleeting breaks in the continuity of thinking. After mowing the lawn, an exhausted man leans his arm on the lawnmower and rests. For a moment or two, his eyes gaze downward and he thinks and feels nothing specific whatsoever. Since for that moment he is not doing anything, we cannot even say that he is making *implicit* thetic assumptions: for that brief period, it is not even an issue whether the grass or even he himself is real. He simply is as he is, with no intentional attitude at all. This does not imply, however, that the experience is devoid of content—even the simplest reflection on that moment would reveal, for example, that he had been gazing on the green of the grass rather than the blue of the sky. Still, the content was not originally an object of consciousness: the grass was there —it assumed meaning—only through reflection on the original experience. In other words, prereflectively there had been a continuity of consciousness or awareness even with the lack of intentional directionality. Even though the reflection on the act later revealed a content of which one had been conscious at the time of the act, there was, prereflectively, no assumptive, unconscious intentional attitude to constitute that content into a meaning-bearing object.

We now see why Dōgen believes without-thinking to be more basic than either thinking or not-thinking. Even though without-thinking—as without-thinking—has no noematic object, as soon as a without-thinking act is reflected upon by thinking, one can isolate various contents (the green grass in the preceding example). These contents are not noematic objects for the original without-thinking act; they are noematic objects for the *reflection* on that act. It is the intentional attitude of the reflection—the constituting of meaning by the noesis of the reflection (an instance of thinking)—that allows the content to surface as noematic objects. The without-thinking act itself made no such objectification and, therefore, had no truly noematic aspect. In other words, the without-thinking act supplies the raw material out of which the later reflective, thinking act develops.

In this sense, the without-thinking mode is more fundamental than the thinking mode: the thinking mode derives its noemata from the nonnoematic contents of a previously experienced without-thinking act. Of course, thinking's dependence on without-thinking for its raw material is only true in the ultimate sense, since a thinking act may also derive its noemata from previous thinking acts, such as trying to recall the lines of a previously memorized poem. But the series can always be traced back to an original without-thinking act.* Where does not-thinking fit into this description? Because thinking is able to reflect on its previous occurrences, the thinking process itself can be objectified. Once it is so objectified, it can become the noematic object of a negation. This negation of the act of thinking is not-thinking.[18]

Consequently, the present moment of experience is always full and self-contained. Only when we engage in thinking or not-thinking and objectify the experience of a past moment does that experience seem limited and capable of being fully analyzed. Dōgen writes: "When one has not yet fully penetrated things *[hō]* personally in one's body-mind, one thinks the truth *[hō]* is already sufficient. If one fulfills things in one's body-mind, one feels something is missing."[19]

---

*In the case of the memorized poem, one first had to learn how to read. To learn to recognize letters, one had to "just gaze" at them at some point and then reflectively learn to associate meanings with their combinations. Without the raw sensory data of without-thinking, thinking would have no ground.

In other words, the more fully one is aware of the prereflective, the more certain one is that the present moment is overbrimming and more than can be circumscribed. Reflective thinking, on the other hand, objectifies the contents of previous experiences, thereby limiting them to a number of significant components. Continuing to reflect, each further bit of analysis uncovers more of the experience and makes it richer. But is it really the past experience that is enriched? When it occurred, the prereflective experience was already self-contained and full; it was only upon *reflection* that it seemed lacking in some way, in need of clarification and enhancement by more reflection. In other words, by retrospectively objectifying the contents of prereflective consciousness (by making them into noemata for thinking), one may lose sight of the fact that without-thinking—as experienced—makes no objectifications at all and, therefore, literally leaves nothing (no-thing) to be clarified, analyzed, or enriched. It is rather the initial *reflective* act that first raises the issue of inadequacy and the need for further clarification. Reflection can only fulfill, clarify, and perfect previous reflections.

All of this implies that without-thinking has some form of its own. To understand this claim, we must deal more directly with the zazen experience itself, especially insofar as it is the epitome of without-thinking. If we can recognize why Dōgen considered zazen to be at once the practice and the realization, the means and the end, we will see why without-thinking requires no enrichment from reflective analysis.

## CULTIVATION-AUTHENTICATION

In the latter part of the *Shōbōgenzō* fascicle "Bendōwa" [A talk on undertaking the way], Dōgen recorded several queries put to him by students and visiting monks. In one case, he was asked a question resembling the one that had so plagued the master himself in his younger days:

Question: As for performing zazen, a person who has not yet authenticated the Buddha's teachings can reach that authentication by undertaking the way [of the Buddhas] in zazen. But if there is someone who has already been able to clarify the Buddha's correct teachings, what does one expect to gain from zazen?

Answer: . . . To think of cultivation-authentication as not a single thing is a view outside the way [of the Buddhas]. In the Buddha's teachings, cultivation-authentication is an identity. Even now, it is the cultivation of authentication. So the very undertaking of the way by a beginner's mind is itself the whole of primordial authentication. For that reason, even in cultivation's being invested with the functioning mind, one is warned not to look expectantly for authentication outside cultivation.[20]

In short, Dōgen rejects the view that zazen is a technique by which one comes to realization. Zazen is not the *cause* of satori; even at that first moment when the student begins to sit in meditation, zazen is already realization. Thus, in referring to enlightenment, Dōgen usually prefers to use the character *shō* ("authentication") rather than *satori* ("realization") or *kaku* ("awakening"). For Dōgen, proper sitting *authenticates* the enlightenment already there. Conversely, the student never reaches the point at which zazen is superseded. To say that one practices zazen in order to become an enlightened person is like saying one practices medicine to become a doctor. To practice medicine is to *be* a doctor. To practice zazen is to *be* enlightened. Enlightenment is not a static state of achievement; it is the active undertaking of the way exemplified in zazen.

Although the unity of cultivation and authentication is verified most directly in the Zen Buddhist's personal experience, Dōgen also tries to describe the nature of zazen in order to build a philosophical foundation for his position. One of Dōgen's descriptive perspectives is gained through his notion of temporality—or, to use his terminology, "being-time." By criticizing our usual understanding of time, Dōgen sets the groundwork for rejecting the idea of practice as preceding and causing authentication. Thus, he says that zazen falls outside the notion of time as past, present, and future:

Because of this, when even just one person, at one time, sits in zazen, he becomes, imperceptively, one with each and all the myriad things, and permeates completely all time, so that within the limitless universe, throughout past, future and present, he is performing the eternal and ceaseless work of guiding beings to enlightenment. It is for each and every thing, one and the same undifferentiated cultivation, and undifferentiated authentication.[21]

Zazen, like without-thinking, precedes the reflective categories of past, present, and future. Dōgen wisely avoids saying that all experience is thereby present experience, for to do so involves a subtle, but dangerous fallacy. If we were to say, for example, that zazen is simply to exist here and now, that statement would be understood within the thinking mode: in maintaining the here and now, one is implicitly negating the *there* and *before/after*, but this is intrinsically problematic. To negate the past and future is to negate the basis of the distinction by which the word *present* has any meaning. Here we see Nāgārjuna's emptiness (as linguistic interdependence) at work.[22] Suppose, then, that here and now is taken to mean the rejection of the past/present/future distinction *in toto*. Then we have merely negated the process of conceptualization itself; we have drifted into not-thinking. As before, a third perspective is needed: one that is outside either the affirmation (thinking) or the negation (not-thinking) of the three related temporal modes of past/present/ future. Since zazen does not reflectively conceptualize the content of experience, these categories do not even arise and cannot, therefore, be either affirmed or denied. It is in this sense that zazen is outside temporal categories; it does not reject temporality itself.

To understand how one lives in the temporal world without depending on temporal concepts, we now investigate the two profiles of time expressed in Dōgen's fascicle "Uji" [Being-time]. In this essay, Dōgen establishes the relationships among three terms: being-time *(uji)*, right-now *(nikon)*, and ranging *(keireki* or *kyōryaku)*. Dōgen's composite term, being-time, signifies the inseparability of beings and times. That is, we experience neither time nor being per se; we experience temporal existence. Depending on one's situation, being-time presents one of two profiles. The first is that of right-now. From one perspective, the Zen practitioner is immersed in the present givenness of experience, without letting it be colored by expectations or past conditioning. Dōgen's idea of the right-now does not imply the notion of logically derived "moments" in an

Abhidharma Buddhist sense of *kṣaṇa;* nor does it imply the
metaphysical idea of an eternal now. It is simply a label for the
appearance of being-time as experienced in our release from considerations of past and present, our total involvement in the nowness
of temporal events. In other situations, however, from another
perspective, time presents a different profile: one of ranging or
flowing. The present is not merely the isolated right-now; it is also
the convergence of past and future. In its profile of ranging, being-
time is not merely unidirectional: "[Being-time] ranges from today
to tomorrow, from today to yesterday, from yesterday to today,
from today to today and from tomorrow to tomorrow. This is so
because ranging itself is the functioning of time."[23]

Throughout the "Uji" fascicle, Dogen plays on the imagery of
climbing to the top of a mountain, suggesting that being atop the
mountain is like the primal experience of temporality: being-time.
Yet, looking around from that mountain top, two possible perspectives can be taken. Each is equally valuable in its own right. One
may either look around and see a series of peaks, each a knife-edge
right-now of being-time; or one may see a vast range of mountains,
the continuous ranging of being-time throughout past, present, and
future. Both these perspectives, Dōgen implies, are equally valid
and, depending on the situation, either might be appropriate. As
long as one does not try to reduce one to the other, or to absolutize
one particular profile of time as its essence, one sees the nature of
temporal events clearly. These events are, of course, always in flux,
and a serious treatment of Dōgen's theory of being-time must consider the importance of impermanence.

Even from its earliest Indian manifestations, Buddhism has
always maintained that everything is in constant flux. For Dōgen,
this principle has importance phenomenologically rather than
metaphysically. As we have seen in the without-thinking mode of
consciousness that is zazen, the disciple overcomes the perception
of things in terms of past/present/future and experiences the
phenomenon just as it is. In other words, if the zazen practitioner
merely receives the unfolding of experience without reflectively
categorizing it, one encounters a stream of ever-changing
phenomena. That is, prereflective consciousness itself involves
*change.*

Dōgen would reject our commonly held notion that change is in the things outside us—that is, a (metaphysical or physical) attribute of objects. Although we often say "everything is changing," the change cannot be located either in the self or in the object. Rather, the change is a constituent of phenomena (dharmas) as they are prereflectively experienced. This leads us to an important Buddhist principle: it is futile to seek a permanently unchanging object, whether it be God, soul, ātman, or an essence that distinguishes one from everyone else. Even if such an object did exist, it would be outside the field of Dōgen's phenomenological reduction; that is, we could never have a direct experience of it. Dōgen expresses this point by analogy:

> When a man goes off in a boat and looks back to see the shoreline, he mistakenly thinks the shore is moving. If he keeps his eyes closely on his boat, he realizes that it is the boat that is advancing. In like manner, when a person (tries to) discern and affirm the myriad dharmas with a confused conception of (his own) body and mind, he mistakenly thinks his own mind and his own nature are permanent. If he makes all his daily deeds intimately his own and returns within himself, the reason that the myriad dharmas are without self [i.e., without a presumed permanent essence] will become clear to him.[24]

In other words, when projecting our experience of change onto some external noumenon, we falsely assume the experiencing self to be unchanging; but when we take the experience of change *as it is* and make no projections beyond what is directly given, there is simply the unending experience of flux.

Thus, things cannot be experienced independently of change, or being independently of time. ABE Masao directly relates Dōgen's views of being-time and universal impermanence:

> Dōgen does not however simply identify being and time. Their common denominator is mutability or impermanence. For Dōgen all beings without exception are impermanent; just because so, all beings are the Buddha nature, for he rejects an immutable Buddha nature beyond impermanence.[25]

In this statement is an explicit reference to Dōgen's reinterpretation of Buddha-nature. Although Buddhism classically maintains the doctrine of impermanence, it also often asserts the idea of universal

Buddha-nature, an essential potentiality of sentient beings to become enlightened. On the surface at least, these two views are at
odds with each other. If there is some unchanging essence called a
Buddha-nature, then indeed there is something permanent and the
doctrine of flux must be abandoned. If the doctrine of flux is strictly maintained, who or what is enlightened?[26]

Dōgen argues that since the prereflective basis of experience is
impermanence, apprehended in zazen as being-time, Buddha-nature
cannot be an immutable essence or potential. Rather, it must be the
experiential presence of impermanence itself. Simply stated, impermanence is not a metaphysical, but a phenomenological, category
for Dōgen: no things are directly experienced as substantial in the
sense of having a changeless essence. Along these lines, Dōgen
reinterprets the classical Chinese doctrine of "all beings have
Buddha-nature" so that it reads "all beings *are* Buddha-nature."[27]
For Dōgen, the Buddha-nature is not a seed of potentiality to be
realized; it is the basic nature of things as experienced. What is this
character? Dōgen says "impermanence is the Buddha-nature."[28] But
impermanence *as experienced* is being-time. When is impermanence
most clearly manifested as impermanence? In zazen. Without the
objectifying activity of thinking, there is in zazen only the experience of universal flux, the flow of temporal events. Therefore, to
practice zazen is to accept Buddha-nature (impermanence) as it
presents itself. To authenticate the presence of Buddha-nature is
enlightenment.

At last we see why cultivation and authentication are the same
for Dōgen. To practice zazen, even for one moment, is to experience directly the universality of being-time, of Buddha-nature, of
impermanence. For that moment, there is nothing more to be
achieved; one has authenticated what is. If zazen is interrupted,
however, if reflective thought (thinking or not-thinking) is superim-
posed onto the experience, temporal categories arise and the
realization is lost. Therefore, while one practices, there is authentication; and if there is authentication, one is practicing. This does
not imply, though, that the Buddha-nature is destroyed by reflective thought. Impermanence is always present, but reflective
thought (insofar as it objectifies and transforms experience into

static, inflexible categories) prevents the Buddha-nature from being experienced as it is: as impermanence.

## GENJŌKŌAN: A CENTRAL CONCEPT

The phrase *genjōkōan* has been differently interpreted by various commentators. As mentioned previously, Dōgen is sensitive to the nuances of language, often playing on the multiple meanings of characters. This is the case here. The first half of the full phrase, *genjō*, has the connotation of "being present already in its completed form." Sometimes *genjō* is translated "manifestation," but this may be misinterpreted as meaning that something previously transcendent becomes immanent. "Being present" has the advantage of utilizing both the spatial (here) and the temporal (now) denotations of the word, but I prefer "presence" because it adds the nuance of special significance.* In any case, it is important that, given Dōgen's emphasis on the prereflective awareness of impermanence, presence is always experienced as a process, not a stasis.

The second half of the phrase, *kōan*, raises further difficulties. There are at least three common interpretations, each illuminating in some respect. One approach is to translate *kōan* literally as "public notice."[29] Given this interpretation, the full phrase would presumably mean "the presence of public (or objective) reality." A second exposition follows an early commentary by Kyōgō, interpreting *kō* as "equality" and *an* as "keeping to one's sphere." This is the line taken by Waddell and Abe in their translation and commentary.[30] Given this rendering, the full phrase, *genjōkōan*, would mean roughly "the individuality of things manifesting themselves equally" (that is, without evaluation, categorization, retrospective objectification). Finally, a third approach is to take *kōan* in its usual meaning in Zen practice—as a paradox given to students as an object of meditation (as in Jōshū's *Mu* koan). Although both Waddell/Abe and Dumoulin reject this analysis,[31] I (along with MASUNAGA Reihō, DESHIMARU Taisen, and KIM Hee-jin)[32] believe it

---

*The verbal form "to presence" is a neologism occasionally required by Dōgen's use of the verb *genjōkōan su*.

cannot be discounted completely. Dōgen himself studied koan practice in China; he even collected and edited a set of koan cases. Furthermore, it is certainly possible he considered "presence itself" *(genjō)* to be a fitting object of meditation, to be penetrated directly without resorting to concepts. In other words, rather than restricting the idea of koan to excerpts from famous Zen dialogues, Dōgen might have considered prereflective experience itself to be a koan. To become directly aware of impermanence, to achieve without-thinking, is itself a paradox in that it requires an attempt to do what must not be willfully attempted. The very practice of zazen itself can be viewed as a koan.

How, then, should we interpret the full phrase *genjōkōan*? All the interpretations point to a similar idea: from the without-thinking attitude of zazen, the ceaseless unfolding of experience is the only reality. As Dumoulin puts it, "This physical world, just as it is, is genuine, patent reality."[33] This accords with what we have said above. For Dōgen, Buddha-nature is impermanence. As directly experienced, impermanence is the "presence of things as they are" *(genjōkōan)*. Again, there is no separation between practice and realization.

Dōgen's characterization of *genjōkōan* is central to understanding his phenomenology of zazen. The unification of cultivation (zazen) and authentication (enlightenment) widens the significance of that phenomenology. That is, if zazen is enlightenment, then a phenomenology of zazen is also a phenomenology of enlightenment itself. As long as one maintains a pure state of without-thinking, one is a Buddha. By this move, Dōgen brings enlightenment closer to us; if we authenticate what we are right here and now, we are enlightened, we are practicing Zen. For Dōgen, enlightenment is neither transcendent nor extraordinary. All that is extraordinary is our persistent refusal to accept our experience for what it is. In fact, our direct experience *as* experienced is not different from the Zen Master's. The difference lies in our placing onto our experience a particular conceptual overlay and taking that to be objectively real in and of itself. For the Zen Master, concepts are only an expression *(dōtoku)* of the occasion *(jisetsu)* as immediately experienced.

Dōgen's phenomenology is thus double-layered. First, there is the prereflective, not yet conceptualized, experience—what we all share, Zen Master and deluded fool alike. Second, there is the expression or characterization of any experience within a particular situation or on a particular occasion. If the speaker or thinker brings no personal, egotistical delusions into the expression, the occasion speaks for itself: the situation alone determines what is said and done. Thus, in the case of the Zen Master, what-is-said is simply what-is. In the case of the deluded person, however, the what-is includes the conceptual baggage with all its affective components—the deluded ideas about the self, thing, time, or whatever—constituting the person's own distortion of what really is. Throughout *Shōbōgenzō*, therefore, Dōgen challenges the reader to investigate whether direct experience really has the form one thinks it does. In the "Being-time" fascicle, for example, Dōgen notes that we often think of time as flying away,[34] but do we really experience this? If we did, there would be a gap between ourselves and time, between things and time. Yet we actually experience ourselves *as* time, things *as* time. Hence, the flying away of time must be, to some degree, a self-delusion: we have convinced ourselves that we have direct experience of something that we do not.

This does not mean there is one and only one correct characterization for a particular thing. Dōgen observes, for example, that the ocean is experienced differently by a fish swimming in it, a heavenly being looking at it from heaven, and a person out at sea in a boat.[35] The occasion or situation is different in each case, so the ocean is legitimately characterized respectively as a "jeweled palace," a "necklace" of shining flecks of light, and a "great circle." The meaning of an expression derives from the context. Can we talk about things independently of perspective? For the fish, the heavenly being, and the person at sea, is there anything in common regarding the directly experienced ocean? Yes. For all of them, prereflectively, there is *genjōkōan:* the presence of the thing as it is. Sometimes Dōgen speaks of this presence adverbially by using a term like *immo*—literally, "being such (as it is)." This term is often improperly construed substantially and metaphysically as "Suchness." *Immo*, though, is not a thing; it is a *way* things are experienced.

Another way of expressing the contextless standpoint is to use an interrogative as an answer. Suppose I were to ask the reader "What is this in front of you?" In the present context, it is a book about Zen Buddhism. In other contexts, it might be a paperweight, kindling, or even a weapon. But what if I were to ask you to answer my question without alluding to the various contexts giving it those meanings? "What is this in front of you?" An appropriate answer might be "The what-is-in-front-of-me." This does not tell us anything new, but it is vitally important to understanding Dōgen's description of without-thinking. Phrases like *being such, the presence of things as they are*, and *the what-is-in-front-of-me* are not meant to be illuminating statements about the nature of the universe. But they do indicate the prereflective experience at the basis of all consciousness, however enlightened or deluded. It is not an objective description so much as a pointer showing us the way to authenticating what we are.

But what are we? In this chapter we have examined Dōgen's basic phenomenology of zazen and seen how the term *genjōkōan* takes us to the utter core of that phenomenology. Indeed, Dōgen himself placed the fascicle "Genjōkōan" at the very beginning of his 75-fascicle version of *Shōbōgenzō*.[36] But what does this phenomenological structure reveal about the nature of the person as understood by Zen Buddhism? Dōgen's views will be explored further in the next chapter.

CHAPTER 7

# Dōgen: Person as Presence

## DŌGEN ON THE SELF

In the last chapter we saw that Dōgen's concept of *genjōkōan* ("the presence of things as they are") is at the heart of his phenomenology of zazen. It is significant, then, that Dōgen's most famous statement on the self comes from the *Shōbōgenzō* fascicle of that same name:

> To model yourself after the way of the Buddhas is to model yourself after yourself. To model yourself after yourself is to forget yourself. To forget yourself is to be authenticated by all things. To be authenticated by all things is to effect the molting of body-mind, both yours and others'. The distinguishing marks of enlightenment dissolve and [the molting of body-mind] causes the dissolving distinguishing marks of enlightenment to emerge continuously.
>
> At first, when you *seek* the truth, you have distanced yourself from its domain. Finally, when the truth is correctly transmitted to you, you are immediately the primordial person.[1]

In this brief passage, Dōgen reveals what it means for one to realize oneself as a person in Zen. Therefore, let us analyze the passage line by line.

*To model yourself after the way of the Buddhas is to model yourself after yourself.*

The phrase "the way of the Buddhas" translates *butsudō*, signifying both the path of discipline taken by the Buddhist sages as well as the Buddha's enlightened mind itself. Hence, the term intrinsically embraces both cultivation and authentication, both disciplined practice and realization. The phrase "to model yourself" translates *narau*, a verb meaning to study or learn something, especially by repeatedly imitating a model or paradigm. Hence, "to model yourself after the way of the Buddhas" refers simultaneously to the novice's effort in undertaking the Zen Buddhist life as well as to the goal of that effort. To understand the full import of Dōgen's statement, then, we must deal with both dimensions: practice and enlightenment.

On the practical side, in hopes of emulating the great religious quest of the Buddhas, the novice strives for *anātman* or "no-ego," but in so doing may reject all aspects of the self. This, in fact, is a rejection of one's own experience—a fall into the nihilism of not-thinking. For Dōgen, however, enlightenment lies in the *authentication* of our own experience. To understand the doctrine of no-ego, therefore, one must not reject (not think about) the self; rather, one must penetrate into its meaning. Thus, Dōgen advises his disciples to find enlightenment not in the teachings of Buddhism nor in the mind of the Zen Master but within themselves. The irony, of course, is that by searching their own experiences, the disciples will eventually discover the truth of the teachings and the Buddha-mind.

From the standpoint of enlightenment, the statement reiterates the idea of *hongaku* ("primordial enlightenment"). Enlightenment lies in the primordially given. To the extent that we do not recognize our enlightenment, we have covered over our prereflective awareness with reflective categories. Therefore, to be in harmony with the way of the Buddhas, we need to model ourselves after our own prereflective experience. This analysis reinforces our interpretation of *genjōkōan* in that Dōgen clearly sees self-awareness to be a fitting object of meditation. The presence of things as they are in Zen practice is itself a koan; one does not have to resort to traditional koans like Jōshū's *"Mu!"*

*To model yourself after yourself is to forget yourself.*

In the without-thinking state of zazen, where is the self? Consider the situation of stubbing your toe and yelling "Ouch!" Who yelled?

Was it a man or a woman? A conservative or liberal? Someone old or young? In looking for oneself as a model from which to learn, one discovers the self to have disappeared. But it does not dissolve into a formless void; it merges into the phenomena of prereflective experience. One might think that one meditates in a quiet place in order to avoid distractions and concentrate on the pure self. But there are no distractions in zazen. A distraction is something present to consciousness but outside of one's desired focus. In zazen, however, presence itself is the sole content: without-thinking has no desired focus. The following anecdote illustrates this point.

A group of Westerners in Kyoto were meeting nightly to meditate in a small, secluded Zen temple. One evening, one of the participants was late and did not have time to eat before the session. About halfway through the sitting period, his stomach began to rumble so loudly its sound reverberated through the meditation hall. The next evening, one of the other participants said to the stomach rumbler, "I hope you ate today. Yesterday, your stomach was so noisy, I couldn't concentrate." The stomach rumbler responded, "Yes, I did eat today. I also arranged for the crickets to be silent and the moon to be dark. So now you should have no distractions at all."

The stomach rumbler was quite right. Zazen does not evaluate sounds or sights as desirable or undesirable. The rumbling of the stomach was part of the presence of things as they are. Caught up in his own preconceptions about meditation as empty tranquillity, the distracted meditator could not forget himself. That is, he could not accept his prereflective experience for what it was—enlightenment.

*To forget yourself is to be authenticated by all things.*

Again Dōgen reminds us that zazen is not devoid of content. As I sit at my desk writing these lines, there is the white page, the yellow pencil in my right hand, the oscillating movement of the hand associated with graphite impressions on the page, the brown desk top, my left hand holding down the pad, the buzz of fluorescent lights above, the sequence of words—thinking them, writing them, reading them as a single, undivided act. These are not merely

things in my experience; they *are* my experience. My self does not
relate to these things; my self *is* these things. The awareness of
this fact is most clear in zazen. At an earlier point in the same
"Genjōkōan" fascicle, Dōgen writes: "To cultivate-authenticate all
things by conveying yourself [to them] is delusion. To cultivate-
authenticate yourself by all things' presenting themselves—this is
realization *[satori].*"²

Primordially, there is simply the process of experience itself: self
and object are subsequent abstractions arising out of that originally
unified experience. Thus, in speaking of things, Dōgen is not sepa-
rating the objects from the experience. "Things" (*hō*, dharmas) are
directly experienced things, given in prereflective experience without the bifurcation between self and object.

As an analogy, we can consider the term *nature* in the sentence
"Nature carefully maintains a balance of opposites (evaporation/
rain, predator/prey, death/life, decay/fertilization, and so on)."
Although this statement is a personification, attributing a will and
intention to nature ("carefully maintains"), this is just metaphor.
*Nature* is an abstraction derived from the observation of many
phenomenal patterns. In fact, it refers to the sum total of the opposites listed in parentheses. To think of nature as having a will and
intentions is the source of misconceptions like nature's being evil or
good, angry or friendly. Dōgen's view of the term *self* is similar.
The word is not meaningless; it generally names a set of processes.
The term is misused, however, when it implies something *behind*
the processes, something initiating those activities rather than being
them.

> *To be authenticated by all things is to effect the molting of body-*
> *mind, both yours and others'.*

As noted in the last chapter, the phrase "molting of body-mind"
was part of Nyojō's exclamation that triggered Dōgen's insight. In
making this phrase, *shinjindatsuraku*, his own technical term,
Dōgen lends it nuances of his own. First, there is the hyphenated
term *body-mind*. Although the phrase *shinjin* could be translated
"body *and* mind," Dōgen often refers explicitly to the "oneness of

body-mind" *(shinjin'ichinyo)*. The distinction between mind and body is often correlated with that between subject and object or mind and matter. None of these categories arise prereflectively, of course. For example, there is just the experience of the chirping cicada without any differentiation between the physical sound waves and my hearing it, between the sensation and the perception, between the somatic and the mental. Although the second part of Dōgen's phrase, *datsuraku*, is sometimes translated "dropping off," the rendering "molting" is preferred since it implies a recurrent event. *Datsuraku* occurs at each sitting—in fact, at each moment of sitting. Thus, the state of zazen is renewed and revitalized at each instant; enlightenment is a continuous process, not a single event.

In the state of without-thinking, there is no separation between body and mind. Since the bifurcation between self and others is not directly experienced either, Dōgen speaks of the molting of the body-mind of others as well. In other words, our isolation from each other arises upon *reflection*. Consider, for example, our awareness of another person's feeling of pain. A medic in the midst of battle might well react spontaneously to the cry of an infantryman in an accompanying bunker. In his prereflective responsiveness, the medic is not conscious of his self effecting changes in an other.

Similarly, walking down the street, I may suddenly respond to a stranger about to slip on the ice, taking hold of his or her arm and performing a rather complex maneuver in stabilizing the other person's balance. At the time of the act, there is no distinguishing self and other or mental intention and physical activity; my body-mind and the body-mind of the other person is a single, complex entity maintaining its own balance. In other words, at the time of the act, we achieve *our* balance point. Like a dance couple, I and the slipping pedestrian are compensating for, and responding to, each other's movements in a completely spontaneous and unreflective manner. Contrast this with a doctor's examination of a patient complaining of a pain in the side. In placing her hand on the patient's side, the doctor may have to *analyze* the patient's cry of pain. Is it appendicitis? Should she operate immediately? Since the situation requires a reflective analysis of the nature and intensity of the patient's pain, the doctor utilizes various conceptual categories: not only etiological, diagnostic, and prognostic ones, but also the distinction between the self who decides what to do and takes responsibility for her actions and the other who will be affected.

There is an important philosophical issue here. As the situation (*jisetsu*) changes, the domain of relevant categories shifts also. The separation between self and other so important to the doctor's situation was not visible in the prereflective response of the medic or in my helping the fellow pedestrian. In other words, the distinction between self and other is not directly experienced in the without-thinking state. This does not mean the distinction is false, but its relevance is restricted to certain situations and areas of discourse. The distinction is germane to discussions of professional ethics, legal responsibility, and physiological diagnosis, for example, but it is wrong to use such categories when describing spontaneous actions and prereflective responses. Even to say that I was beyond the separation of self and other in helping the pedestrian is misleading. Such a characterization implicitly assumes that those categories are primary and that I temporarily transcended them. This is to confuse without-thinking with not-thinking. It is not that I did not think of self and other. Rather, without thinking, there is no self or other.

*The distinguishing marks of enlightenment dissolve and [the molting of body-mind] causes the dissolving distinguishing marks of enlightenment to emerge continuously.*

This striking statement is not as paradoxical as it might at first seem. As a continuous state of authentication, enlightenment involves the recurrent return to what is now being directly experienced. The body-mind that has just encountered the presence of things as they are is molted so that the current presence can be encountered anew without prejudice. Each moment of enlightenment is a renewal: enlightenment is a presently ongoing process, and the enlightenment that was a moment ago dissolves into the enlightenment of right now. Thus, as soon as the authenticating moment of enlightenment occurs, as soon as its distinguishing traces are visible, it passes away to make room for the next authenticating moment.

*At first, when you seek the truth, you have distanced yourself from its domain. Finally, when the truth is correctly transmitted to you, you are immediately the primordial person.*

The word *truth* is *hō* or dharma. Its meaning encompasses directly experienced phenomena as well as the teachings of Buddhism—the truth of things as well as the truth of ideas. The contrast is the novice's search for external truth as opposed to truth's discovery within one's own prereflective (primordial) experience. Dōgen's "primordial person" *(honbunnin)* is suggestive. Enlightenment is the direct recognition of what one most fundamentally is: the purity, unity, and responsiveness of prereflective experience. In effect, this is Dōgen's final elaboration on the statement "to model yourself after the way of the Buddhas is to model yourself after yourself." It is Dōgen's equivalent of Rinzai's true person of no status, of Enō's original face before one's parents were born, and even, as suggested in the Preface, of Socrates' knowing oneself. To appreciate the practical significance of Dōgen's view of the person, we now turn to its ethical implications.

## DŌGEN ON GOOD AND EVIL

Our discussion of Japanese Zen Buddhism would be incomplete if we did not address the moral dimension of its teachings. Dōgen's view on good and evil is best expressed in his "Shoakumakusa," another fascicle of *Shōbōgenzō* and one of the most profound discussions of morality in Mahāyāna Buddhism. In this work, Dōgen tries to resolve a conflict within the Zen tradition. On the one hand, Zen wishes to be traditionally Buddhist; this entails recognition of various moral edicts passed down through the centuries. On the other hand, as an offshoot of the Mahāyāna wing of Buddhism and, in particular, of Nāgārjuna's viewpoint, Zen considers distinctions such as that between good and evil to be relative rather than absolute. Therefore, Dōgen wants to show how it is possible to affirm traditional moral exhortations while simultaneously denying the absoluteness of the distinction between good and evil. His analysis builds on his phenomenology of zazen and his understanding of the person.

As a focal point in working out his position, Dōgen again resorts to a highly unorthodox interpretation of a classical Chinese scriptural passage:[3]

| Japanese Pronunciation | Traditional Interpretation |
|---|---|
| Shoakumakusa | Do no evil; |
| Shuzenbugyō | Do good; |
| Jijōgoi | Purify your own intentions; |
| Zeshobukkyō | This is the teaching of all Buddhas. |

Dōgen's Interpretation

The nonproduction of evil,
The performance of good,
The purification of one's own intentions:
This is the teaching of all Buddhas.

As the scheme indicates, Dōgen's basic strategy is to regard this passage not as an ethical imperative but as a description of the ideal state of mind. In so doing, the discussion shifts from moral rectitude to authentication.

To open his commentary, Dōgen assures us that "*shoakumakusa, shuzenbugyō, jijōgoi*" is the teaching of all Buddhas and only a devil would say otherwise. Yet evil is relative; what is evil at one time, in one place, may not be evil in a different time, a different place. The key to overcoming this apparent contradiction is in understanding the full import of the phrase:

> Know that it is the correct teaching of the Buddha when the phrase *shoakumakusa* is heard. Ordinary people at first construe this as "do no evil" *[shoakutsukurukoto nakare]*, but it is not what they make it out to be. One hears it thus when one is taught about enlightenment as suited for exposition. So heard, it is an expression in which unexcelled enlightenment is verbal. Since it is already the words of enlightenment, it is the stating of enlightenment. In hearing the unexcelled enlightenment be expounded, things are turned around: the resolve to do no evil continues as the act of not producing evil. When it comes

to be that evils are no longer produced, the efficacy of one's cultivation is immediately presencing *[genjōsu]*. This presence exhaustively presences all places, worlds, times and phenomena [hō, dharmas] as its domain, the domain which takes for itself nonproduction *[makusa]*.[4]

The term *nonproduction* translates Dōgen's special use of *makusa*. The character *SA (tsukuru)* can mean "to do," but it has connotations of making, creating, or producing. Dōgen's point, then, is that in saying "*shoakumakusa*," the implication is that one produces no evil. But, given Dōgen's overall characterization of consciousness, if one produces no categories to superimpose onto prereflective experience, there can be no evils at all. Hence, nonproduction itself entails the nonproduction of evil. "It is not that there are no evils, but it is only that they are nonproduction." In fact, Dōgen goes on to say that all things—pine trees, chrysanthemums, the utensils of the monastery, even the self *(jiko)*—are "neither being *[u]* nor nonbeing *[mu]*; they are nonproduction."

This characterization of nonproduction as neither affirming nor negating is obviously reminiscent of our discussion of without-thinking. Since, following Nāgārjuna's argument, terms like good and evil are interdependent concepts, they operate on the level of thinking, but nonproduction is prior to such categorizations. In this regard, to say "the nonproduction of evil" *(shoakumakusa)* is superfluous; "nonproduction" *(makusa)* is sufficient. Upon first hearing the phrase "*shoakumakusa*," the novice takes it to be an exhortation to do no evil. In so doing, the disciple undertakes the Buddhist disciplines, but then, as the person is spiritually transformed, the words *state* the enlightenment of the disciple. That is, it is no longer an imperative; it is now a description of without-thinking. As Dōgen puts it, "the efficacy of one's cultivation is immediately presencing."

The term *nonproduction* may seem negative and passive. Like the Taoist *wu-wei*, however, without-thinking is no retreat from the world; it is the *participation* in the presence of things as they are, an idea emphasized by Dōgen's discussion of the second line, *shuzenbugyō*. Dōgen makes three points: (1) good, like evil, is relative and dependent on the situation; (2) one can simply speak of performance *(bugyō)* instead of the performance of good deeds *(shuzenbugyō)*; (3) insofar as performance makes no distinction between good and evil and neither affirms nor denies such categories, it also is *genjōkōan*—"the cause and effect of this 'good' are, similarly, the *genjōkōan* that is *bugyō*."[5]

Since nonproduction and performance are both *genjōkōan*, they must be equivalent. Dōgen brings them together in the third phrase of the passage: *jijōgoi*, "the purification of one's own intentions." Dōgen, by the way, admonishes us not to objectify the terms *intentions* and *one's own*. Through keeping one's own mind pure, through the experience of without-thinking grounded in zazen, there is nonproduction (that is, there is no creation of thought objects), yet there is full performance (that is, reality is the ever renewing process of the presence of things as they are).

To see how Dōgen's play on words expresses a profound point, we can imagine his treatment of the biblical "Thou shalt not kill." Dōgen might argue that one first takes this to be a divine imperative, "Do not kill," and thus one undertakes a religiously moral life. After some time, however, the efficacy of one's spiritual cultivation is such that one is no longer capable of murder. At that point, one suddenly sees the phrase as a description: "[You are such a person that] you will not kill." In other words, the phrase "Thou shalt not kill" always has spiritual force, but its meaning must be continually authenticated by the person from his or her own spiritual situation. As Dōgen would put it, to say that one supersedes such phrases would be "a teaching of Mara [the devil]." This point is exemplified by the anecdote concluding the fascicle "Shoaku-makusa."

As a novice, the famous Chinese poet, HAKU Kyoi (Ch: Po Chü-i), asked Zen Master Dōrin (Ch: Tao-lin) the true meaning of Buddhism. Dōrin replied, *"shoakumakusa, shuzenbugyō."* When the poet retorted that even a three-year-old might understand that, the master explained: "Though a three-year-old baby might express it, [even] an eighty-year-old man cannot practice it." Of course, Haku had taken the phrase to be a simple imperative. Nevertheless, he should have seen the truth in it for him: "Even if he [Dōrin] had admonished against evils and had advocated good in a contrived way, the presence *[genjō]* would still necessarily be *makusa.*"

In other words, if the poet could simply accept Dōrin's utterance, even if he took it to be a simple imperative, he would have begun the discipline with earnestness and would have reached deeper and deeper interpretations as his own spiritual situation evolved. What Haku could not confront was the presence of the *makusa*, however he understood it at that time. He could not, or would not, authenticate the presence of things as they are—in this case, the *makusa* as an imperative. This is why Dōgen insists that even the mind of the serious novice who earnestly confronts his or her own experience is the presence of Buddhist realization. Even though one may not yet understand the whys and wherefores of zazen, from the standpoint of the Zen Master even the very first practice is already authentication.

This investigation of the moral dimension of Zen Buddhism may still leave the Western moralist uneasy. Zen has thrown us into the midst of a relativism. Unlike Joseph Fletcher's situation ethics, though, there is apparently no overriding criterion such as *agapē* to guide the individual in a moral dilemma. In the Zen view there is literally nothing to hold onto; to be responsible is simply to be responsive. Lest this lack of fixed criteria become a serious stumbling block to the Western reader, some further cross-cultural comparisons should prove of value.

## THE PHILOSOPHICAL SIGNIFICANCE OF DŌGEN'S ETHICS

As part of the Mahāyāna tradition, Zen holds that compassion (Skrt: *karunā*) is fundamentally equivalent to intuitive wisdom *(prajñā)*. The preceding chapter argued that one cannot analyze away prereflective experience. Insofar as the noetic or "act" aspect of without-thinking is fundamentally different from the noetic aspects of thinking and not-thinking, a reflective, conceptual reduction of prereflective experience will rob it of its intensity, spontaneity, and equanimity. The Confucian Mencius wrote movingly of our underlying humaneness (Ch: *jên*). Who would not, Mencius argued, feel a spontaneous urge to help a baby about to fall into a well? Of course, this does not mean that everyone would actually try to help. If the baby were the crown prince and the observer were the next in line to the throne, for example, one might repress the compassionate urge and let the baby die. The point is that only *after* distinctions are introduced is that urge thwarted. Thinking not only fails to grasp the true nature of prereflective compassion; ᶜ often *obstructs* the expression of compassion.

But must thinking always function in this way? The Golden Rule, for example, makes distinctions between self and other so that the differences between self and other can be broken down. Western ethical systems generally attempt to neutralize selfishness by developing counterconcepts of morality, righteousness, fairness, *agapē*, and so on. Zen, more radically, eliminates selfishness by modeling oneself after oneself and, therefore, forgetting oneself. For Zen, compassion and intuitive wisdom are the same because both radiate from the pre-ego mode of without-thinking. Only if the ego has been extirpated can there be compassion without distinctions and wisdom without presuppositions. In contrast, Western ethics has generally developed a thinking or not-thinking approach to morality. By developing conceptual checks and balances on egotism, the selfish ego is overcome either by subjecting it to a higher principle as in Kant's categorical imperative (a thinking mode) or by opening it up to a new dimension as in Buber's I-Thou relationship. (Insofar as this relationship consciously neither affirms nor denies ego but deliberately transcends ego, it bears some relationship to the not-thinking mode.)

It is not our task here to decide whether the Zen view of morality is better or worse than Western views. Our only point is to show the Zen view to be neither primitive nor mystically obscure. Furthermore, it presents a contribution to further considerations of the moral dimension of humankind, East or West. If Dōgen is correct in believing compassion, equanimity, and true selflessness are available to us only prereflectively, then Western accounts of morality must consider more seriously the importance of the prereflective aspect of experience.[6] Even if Western philosophers continue to maintain that consciousness should always remain primarily rational and conceptually oriented, the *capacity* to respond prereflectively should still be nourished. Otherwise, we will lose, along with that capacity, the possibility of being truly compassionate, selfless, and spontaneously moral. In light of Dōgen's account of the meanings of self and morality, we can now focus directly on what it means to be a person in Zen.

## THE PERSON AS PRESENCE

By rejecting the dichotomy between cultivating practice and direct authentication, Dōgen has depicted a dynamic and positive image of the person. Like all traditional Buddhists, he has rejected the idea of a substantial ego underlying the process of experience. There is no soul, no independently existing mind, no "ghost in the machine," as Gilbert Ryle would put it. Nor is there an empirical self that can be the object of perceptual experience. What is intriguing about Dōgen's position, however, is that this rejection of ego does not render self-examination meaningless or unnecessary. While there is no experiencer to reflect on, experience itself is a reflexive process. Not directed by an outside agency, experience directs, or constitutes, itself. Although this notion may seem paradoxical, it is nonetheless crucial to understanding Dōgen. Let us approach it in two different ways.

### Self-constitution as Self-control

First, it is a universal aspect of human experience that, at least sometimes and in some respects, we are certain we can control our own activity. That is, under the proper conditions, we believe we can affect not only our behavior but also, as the Stoics pointed out, our attitudes and emotions as well. Let us put aside for now the issue of whether our belief is actually justified. We are concerned here only with the phenomenological issue of whether Dōgen's view of the person can satisfactorily describe how we come by such beliefs, even though we presumably have no independently existing ego. That is, if the person is nothing more or less than the flow of experiential events, how is it that we sometimes feel there is an "I" controlling that process?

It is important to remember, first of all, that consciousness is reflexive. This reflexivity allows us to be aware of our experiences following one another—not only in trains of thought but in patterns of emotion as well. Thus, in the intellectual sphere, we are aware that when something unexpected and troublesome arises, we naturally inquire into the cause of the situation. Similarly, in the emotional sphere, we recognize that an episode of anger in the morning makes us more likely to be annoyed by an innocuous situation in the afternoon. In everyday life, this means we are apt to make a computational error in our checkbook when the mind is on something else. Even in such ordinary events, we are also aware of the interrelated patterns of our experience and we often adapt ourselves to them. Recognizing our lack of concentration, for example, we might double- or triple-check the subtraction in the checkbook.

The issue at stake is this: who or what is doing the adapting? The experiencing process itself. How? By disengaging itself from the contents of experiences that were formerly, but are no longer, directly experienced. Thus, the person returns to the source of his or her experience: the immediate situation of the presence of things as they are *(genjōkōan)*. Since one is now balancing a checkbook, one attends to that. In other words, there is a return from thinking to a state of without-thinking.

This without-thinking is only a center point, and it might well evoke a thinking act as the appropriate response to the situation *(jisetsu)*. In attending to the checkbook, for example, computational thinking is required. Even a not-thinking act might be suitable in some situation, as in enduring a sharp pain. In any case, without-thinking is the basis of every thinking or not-thinking act. When operative in such a fashion, experience is grounded in its most direct contact with concrete reality. In a similar vein, Ricoeur sees Husserl's phenomenology as a restatement of the primacy of our direct perception of things:

> The first truth of the world is not the truth of mathematical physics but the truth of perception; or rather the truth of science is erected as a superstructure upon a first foundation of presence and existence, that of the world lived through perceptually. . . .

> There [in Husserl's *Ideas II*] it appears clearly that "constituting" is not constructing, even less creating, but rather the unfolding of the intendings of consciousness which are merged together in the natural, unreflective, naive, grasp of a thing.[7]

As an organic, living system, the experiential process has a natural tendency toward simplicity and the conservation of energy. Thus, without-thinking gives the impression of spontaneity, naturalness, and quiescence. The return to without-thinking is a natural process needing no external agency. Since zazen is the epitome of without-thinking, it sets the standard for the direct experience grounding all reflective thinking and not-thinking. The more one practices zazen, the more aware one is of the quiescence of without-thinking and the more readily one returns to it even when not sitting.

## Self-constitution as Weltanschauung

A second way of talking about the self-constituting of experience is in terms of the interdependence of attitudes and objects. Our attitude toward the world affects what we choose to focus on in that world; what we focus on affects our attitude. In other words, we bestow significance on various objects in our experiential field and the sum of those meanings coalesce into an interpretation of the world. This *Weltanschauung* then affects what we perceive as significant or meaningful. In short, we bring not only a perspective but also a slant to our future interpretation. The experiential process is structured in such a way that it literally rejects part of itself; what we experience prereflectively is screened out by the presuppositions of our reflectively constructed worldview. Experience, therefore, turns against its own drive toward unification, simplicity, and directness; it lives an internal lie. The reflective experience cuts itself off from its prereflective roots: one claims a direct experience of things not prereflectively experienced, and one claims no experience of things that are, in fact, immediately experienced.

This internal conflict can be suddenly resolved and the inauthentic *Weltanschauung* destroyed, however, when one comes face to face with the actual nature of prereflective experience. Zazen is the primary way of doing this, but when the person's viewpoint is so rigid that he or she cannot even sit without thinking, extraordinary techniques may be used by the Zen Master, techniques we examine in the next chapter. When zazen is practiced properly, however, it is itself the direct authentication of what simply is. Given this indubitable, direct encounter, experience constitutes itself in a new way, grounding itself once again in the primordial givenness of prereflection. Situations (jisetsu) are then directly apprehended and the response is more intimately connected with the presently experienced content.

## Dōgen's Standpoint

We can now succinctly characterize Dōgen's standpoint. First, one must accept oneself as one sees oneself. If you think there is a substantial self, investigate that self. Where is its presence? How does it function? If you understand shoakumakusa as "do no evil," accept that interpretation and live by it. If you think time flies away, examine your own experience to authenticate its being so. Do not accept any view on mere faith; authenticate it within your own experience. If you feel anger, investigate it: what is its presence? Is it a response to what now confronts you or is it a residue of some past experience? Second, aware that one can construct a worldview out of self-delusions, one must check for such delusions by comparing them against what appears prereflectively. In zazen there is no room for delusion since there is no reflection. Just sitting (shikantaza) is, consequently, the central experience in the Zen Buddhist's life. The pure cultivating practice of zazen is itself authentication. Third, act. When one is grounded in zazen, without-thinking operates as the direct source of thinking or not-thinking. Unless it is the motive force behind activity, without-thinking cannot infuse thinking and not-thinking. The presence (genjō) of every occasion (jisetsu) is the koan. Each life situation must first be confronted directly on its own terms, without coloration by reflection. Then, and only then, can one be truly responsive and, consequently, spontaneously moral. Only after the situation has been clearly apprehended will it be clear whether, and in what way, reflection is necessary.

But what if the unreflective response is rage? Accept the fact that rage has been elicited and examine it. Does it arise from the situation itself or from preconceptions underlying one's conceptually constructed worldview? Appeal to the touchstone of Zen practice. It might be the rage of a peeved and selfish child or it might be the rage of Jesus in the temple. No ethical principles or reflective weighing of values come into play. The authentication of one's act is ultimately internal and prereflective. It is this act that makes one a *person* in the Zen Buddhist sense of the word.

In concluding our consideration of Dōgen, let us examine a poem he wrote shortly before his death. In this poem about the nature of life, we sense Dōgen's ability to capture the vitality of the briefest moment of experience and reveal its completeness:

| | |
|---|---|
| *Yononaka wa* | Being-in-the-world: |
| *Nan ni tatoen* | To what might it be compared? |
| *Mizutori no* | Dwelling in the dewdrop |
| *Hashi furu tsuyu ni* | Fallen from a waterfowl's beak, |
| *Yadoru tsukikage*[8] | The image of the moon. |

# CHAPTER 8

# Hakuin: The Psychodynamics of Zen Training

Zazen is the central practice of Zen Buddhism but, as readers of popular books on the subject are well aware, Zen is also characterized by other practices, seemingly bizarre, such as striking, shouting, and use of the koan. Although many of these activities, especially koan training, are identified with the Rinzai form of Zen, this sectarian identification is as recent as the last century or two. Dōgen himself collected a group of three hundred "cases" or koans, and it seems probable that he used koan practice with at least some of his students. Furthermore, even among contemporary Sōtō Masters, there are those who use koans with at least some disciples. There are also probably some Rinzai Masters who do not, formally at least, use the traditional koan practice for all their students. In short, neither Rinzai nor Sōtō Zen is quite as monolithic as some commentators have implied.

I do not mean to identify Sōtō and Rinzai Zen. These two orders of Zen Buddhism are distinct in many ways, particularly in their practical training. Rinzai stresses the personal identity crisis resolved only by the achievement of satori, a sudden enlightenment. Sōtō on the other hand, because of its emphasis on the dynamics of zazen practice, is often referred to as the gradual enlightenment school. As our comparison will show, the Rinzai Master Hakuin centers his discussion on realization whereas Dōgen, traditionally the founder of Sōtō Zen, concentrates on the unity of cultivation and authentication. Some see this difference as one of perspective: Dōgen speaking from the enlightened viewpoint of the Zen Master; Hakuin, as if from the unenlightened viewpoint of his students. In other words, a Rinzai Master might agree with Dōgen that when zazen is practiced perfectly there is complete realization, but he might question whether the identification between cultivation and authentication is intelligible to the student who has not yet sat in true zazen. In theory, both Rinzai and Sōtō Zen agree on the goal —without-thinking—but they differ as to how it is best achieved in actual practice.

Since Zen practices are integral to the training of disciples and are based on specific insights concerning the goals of that training, it will be helpful to examine the career of the most influential Rinzai Master in Japanese history in a way that reveals a rationale not confined to that particular form of Zen Buddhism. Hence we begin with a brief account of the spiritual odyssey of HAKUIN Ekaku (1685-1768).

Poet, painter, and calligrapher as well as Zen Master, Hakuin was more mystical than philosophical, more aesthetic than logical, more active than reflective. Whereas Dōgen was intent on the phenomenological explication of consciousness, in both its prereflective and reflective forms, Hakuin was concerned with the dynamics of psychological struggle—the pains, frustrations, and ultimately the joy encountered on the spiritual path. Hence, for observing the development of the person in Zen practice, there is no better commentator than Hakuin. Along with extraordinary insight into human psychology, he had the ability to describe his own spiritual progress, both the despair and the ecstasy. This vividness sets Hakuin's account apart from most other Chinese and Japanese Zen writings, in which typically only an isolated phrase or two records the great masters' spiritual experiences.

## HAKUIN'S ROAD TO REALIZATION

As a child of seven or eight, Hakuin tells us, he was deeply moved by a fire and brimstone speech delivered by a priest of Nichiren Buddhism. Guilty of the "heinous sins" of killing insects and small birds, the young Hakuin was convinced he would burn in the Eight Hot Hells. Consequently, even at this early age, Hakuin became preoccupied with spiritual roads to salvation. The fear of burning in hell so tormented him in those early years that once, when fire-wood was being burned to heat the bathwater, the crackling of logs reminded him of hell and his screams "resounded through the neighborhood."[1] At that point, Hakuin vowed to become a monk. His parents, quite understandably, forbade his leaving home at such a young age, but when he was fifteen he finally received their permission to become a monk in the local Zen temple, Shōin-ji. Here we can observe the earliest stage in the development of a characteristic Zen personality—the deep dissatisfaction with secular life and the determination to undertake the religious discipline.

Hakuin's early years of Zen training were not rewarding, however. His practice seemed to him aimless and unproductive. At the age of nineteen, he read the story of how the Chinese Zen Master Gantō (Ch: Yen-t'ou) had been brutally murdered by bandits and how the monk's cries were supposedly heard for miles. For someone who had turned to Zen as a means of escaping suffering, this story was completely demoralizing:

> If such a thing could happen to a man who was like a unicorn or a phoenix among monks, a dragon in the sea of Buddhism, how was I to escape the staves of the demons of hell after I died? What use was there in studying Zen? What a fraud Buddhism! How I regretted that I had cast myself into this band of strange and evil men. What was I to do now? So great was my distress that for three days I could not eat and for a long time my faith in Buddhism was completely lost. . . . It seemed much better to read lay works, to amuse myself with poetry and prose, and thus to a small degree to alleviate my distress.[2]

Turning away from Zen, Hakuin studied the great literary works of China and Japan. Wandering from temple to temple, he eventually met the poet Baō, under whose guidance he developed literary skills he would later utilize as a Zen Master.

One day, while Baō was airing his scrolls outdoors, Hakuin mused over the course of his life. He decided to give religious discipline another try. But which discipline? Buddhism? Taoism? Confucianism? Saying a prayer, he arbitrarily picked up one of the scrolls. It happened to be a collection of Zen stories from Ming dynasty China. Hakuin was deeply moved by the story of the Zen

Master SEKISŌ Soen (Ch: SHIH-SHUANG Ch'u-yüan), who meditated
in zazen day and night and kept an awl beside him at all times, to
be used in stabbing his own flesh should he start to doze. This example of bold determination inspired Hakuin to press on in his
spiritual quest. Concentrating on the *Mu* koan of Jōshū, Hakuin experienced his first glimmer of enlightenment at the age of twenty-
four:

> Night and day I did not sleep! I forgot both to eat and rest. Suddenly
> a great doubt manifested itself before me. It was as though I were
> frozen solid in the midst of an ice sheet extending tens of thousands of
> miles. A purity filled my breast and I could neither go forward nor
> retreat. To all intents and purposes I was out of my mind and the *Mu*
> alone remained. Although I sat in the Lecture Hall and listened to the
> Master's lecture, it was as though I were hearing a discussion from a
> distance outside the hall. At times it felt as though I was floating
> through the air.
>
> This state lasted for several days. Then I chanced to hear the sound
> of the temple bell and I was suddenly transformed. It was as if a sheet
> of ice had been smashed or a jade tower had fallen with a crash.
> Suddenly I returned to my senses. I felt then that I had achieved the
> status of Yen-t'ou, who through the three periods of time encountered
> not the slightest loss (although he had been murdered by bandits). All
> my former doubts vanished as though ice had melted away. In a loud
> voice I called: "Wonderful! Wonderful! There is no cycle of birth and
> death through which one must pass. There is no enlightenment which
> one must seek. . . ." My pride soared up like a majestic mountain, my
> arrogance surged forward like the tide. Smugly I thought to myself:
> "In the past two or three hundred years no one could have accom-
> plished such a marvelous breakthrough as this."[3]

This passage is notable for Hakuin's account of the Great Doubt
*(daigi)* or the Ball of Doubt *(gidan)*. Hakuin came to believe this to
be the necessary first stage toward realization, and he later considered it one of his primary responsibilities as a Zen Master to
effect it in his disciples. He also maintained that the depth of the
eventual realization was equal to the intensity of the Great Doubt
preceding it: "If your doubt measures ten degrees so will the
enlightenment."[4]

In other words, the more diligently the student practices, the more he or she will abandon former ways of experiencing and the deeper will be the realization. Furthermore, through the manifestation of the Great Doubt, enlightenment is assured: "Once the Great Doubt arises, out of a hundred who practice, one hundred will achieve a breakthrough; and of one thousand, a thousand will break through."⁵ This breakthrough is sometimes called the Great Death *(daishi)*. In the following passage, Hakuin gives another account of the Great Doubt and its resolution. Here we can see why he used the term Great Death:

It you are not a hero who has truly seen into his own nature, don't think it is something that can be known easily. If you wish accordance with the true, pure non-ego, you must be prepared to let go your hold when hanging from a sheer precipice, to die and return again to life. Only then can you attain to the true ego of the four Nirvana virtues.

What is "to let go your hold when hanging from a sheer precipice"? Supposing a man should find himself in some desolate area where no man has ever walked before. Below him are the perpendicular walls of a bottomless chasm. His feet rest precariously on a patch of slippery moss, and there is no spot of earth on which he can steady himself. He can neither advance nor retreat; he only faces death. The only things he has on which to depend are a vine that he grasps by the left hand and a creeper that he holds with his right. His life hangs as if from a dangling thread. If he were suddenly to let go, his dried bones would not even be left.

So it is with the study of the Way. If you take up one koan and investigate it unceasingly your mind will die and your will will be destroyed. . . . It is as though a vast, empty abyss lay before you, with no place to set your hands and feet. You face death and your bosom feels as though it were afire. Then suddenly you are one with the koan, and both body and mind are cast off. This is known as the time when the hands are released over the abyss. Then when suddenly you return to life, there is the great joy *[daikangi]* of one who drinks the water and knows for himself whether it is hot or cold. . . . You must push forward relentlessly and with the help of this complete concentration you will penetrate without fail to the basic source of your own nature.⁶

This final, complete letting go of the ego is the Great Death. We will return to the Great Doubt and Great Death in the next section; here we need only note that by Hakuin's own description of his initial realization, his "pride soared up like a majestic mountain, [his] arrogance surged forward like the tide." Obviously, he did not realize he had not yet fully experienced the egolessness of the Great Death. He was to be subjected to a rather harsh lesson. In the next encounter, we see Hakuin's new master skillfully using some of the more bizarre techniques of Zen training in order to deepen his disciple's realization.

Convinced of his enlightenment, Hakuin traveled to Shinano to have the Zen Master SHŌJU Rōjin (or DŌKYŌ Etan, 1642–1721) authenticate the depth of his realization. Hakuin presented Shōju with a verse he had written expressing his understanding (one of the traditional ways in which a disciple may display his insight to a Zen Master). A dialogue ensued:

The Master, holding my verse in his left hand, said to me: "This verse is what you have learned from study. Now show me what your intuition has to say," and he held out his right hand.

I replied: "If there were something intuitive that I could show you, I'd vomit it out," and I made a gagging sound.

The Master said: "How do you understand Chao-chu's [Jp: Jōshū's] *Mu?*" [This is the koan which had raised the Great Doubt in Hakuin.]

I replied: "What sort of place does *Mu* have that one can attach arms and legs to it?"

The Master twisted my nose with his fingers and said: "Here's someplace to attach arms and legs." I was non-plussed and the Master gave a hearty laugh. "You poor hole-dwelling devil!" he cried. I paid him no attention and he continued: "Do you think somehow that you have sufficient understanding?"

I answered: "What do you think is missing?"

Then the Master began to discuss the koan that tells of Nanch'üan's [Jp: Nansen's] death. I clapped my hands over my ears and started out of the room. The Master called after me: "Hey monk!" and when I turned to him he added: "You poor hole-dwelling devil!" From then on, almost every time he saw me, the Master called me a "poor hole-dwelling devil."[7]

Thus, Shōju rejected Hakuin's realization. Perhaps his supposed insight was nihilistic; perhaps he was too egocentric and arrogant. Dumoulin comments on the appropriateness of Shōju's epithet for Hakuin: "Like the devil in the dark dungeon, so his mind without his knowing was still imprisoned in his own ego."[8]

In any case, Hakuin meditated persistently on his new koan (Nansen's death), only to be rejected by Shōju again and again. Once, Hakuin explains, he presented another verse: once more he was rebuked, and when he returned the rebuke, Shōju grabbed him, beat him with his fists, and threw him off the veranda into the mud:

> I lay stretched out in the mud as though dead, scarcely breathing and almost unconscious. I could not move; meanwhile the Master sat on the veranda roaring with laughter. After a short while I regained consciousness, got up, and bowed to the Master. My body was bathed in perspiration. The Master called out to me in a loud voice: "You poor hole-dwelling devil!"[9]

This episode only spurred on Hakuin all the more, but his efforts were to no avail. Once, full of despair, he went begging in the village. Angered at the sight of the gloomy monk begging for food, a householder rendered Hakuin unconscious by beating him over the head with a broomstick. When he recovered consciousness, he suddenly experienced realization. Clapping his hands and laughing, Hakuin appeared to be mad and the villagers all ran back to their homes. On the way back to the temple, an old man offered him tea and rice, commenting, "The honorable bonze was like dead."[10] Indeed Hakuin *had* experienced the Great Death. Upon relating his experience to Shōju, "the Master neither approved nor denied what I said, but only laughed pleasantly. But from this time on he stopped calling me a 'poor hole-dwelling devil'."[11]

Hakuin had a series of more subtle realizations throughout his remaining fifty-eight years. Speaking of these later experiences, he said: "At times there are words to express such experiences, but to my regret at other times there are none. It was as though I were walking about in the shadow cast by a lantern."[12] The depth of Hakuin's attainment was such that almost anything could be the occasion for a further realization. He once had an enlightenment experience while reading a poem and, at another time, while hearing the snow fall as he was sitting in meditation. At the age of thirty-two Hakuin returned to Shōin-ji, the temple he had first entered at fifteen. Restoring it from disrepair, he pursued a vigorous life of teaching. By no means did Hakuin limit his teaching to monks, however. He also preached among the people and in his letters we can see his great compassion for the layman's spiritual problems as well, urging them to practice Zen in their everyday activities. In the same way, Hakuin would chastise his monks for lapsing into "dead sitting" *(shiza)* and for seeking enlightenment through "silent illumination Zen" *(mokushō zen)*.[13] Zen, according to Hakuin, is not only carried out in a quiet place separated from the activities of the world; it must permeate one's existence as the source of everything one does. This active participation in worldly affairs Hakuin called "[meditative] diligence in the midst of activity" *(dōchū no kufū)*. Hakuin himself once suffered from a type of nervous breakdown called the "Zen sickness":

> Trivial and mundane matters pressed against my chest and a fire mounted in my heart. I was unable to enter wholeheartedly into the active practice of Zen. My manner became irrascible and fears assailed me. Both my mind and body felt continually weak, sweat poured ceaselessly from my armpits, and my eyes constantly filled with tears. My mind was in a continual state of depression and I made not the slightest advance toward gaining the benefits that result from the study of Buddhism.[14]

The cause of all this trouble, Hakuin believed, was that he had ignored the care of his body, mistakenly believing that Zen meditation had to be carried out by the forceful rejection of all worldly concerns. The ideal, Hakuin maintained, is to be neither seeking nor denying the mundane realm. This is true meditation in the midst of activity:

> What is this true meditation? It is to make everything: coughing, swallowing, waving the arms, motion, stillness, words, action, the evil and the good, prosperity and shame, gain and loss, right and wrong, into one single koan.[15]

Thus, for Hakuin's traditional koans as well as for Dōgen's *gen-jōkōan*, each and every activity of daily life is a spiritual concern. Whether one is sitting in zazen or doing bureaucratic paperwork for the shogun, Hakuin advises a deep psychophysical concentration, the mind focused on the koan and the breath centered in the abdomen. Such a way of life is open to anyone in any circumstance. Hakuin himself manifested his own compassion and insight in everything he did, whether training disciples, writing letters to laymen, painting, or writing poetry. His influence on Zen has been so powerful that all modern Rinzai Masters trace their lineage directly to him.[16] He is known as the "greatest sage in five hundred years" and the "patriarch who revised Zen."

## THE GREAT DOUBT AND THE GREAT DEATH

Because Hakuin considered the Great Doubt to be a necessary stage in the path to realization, the question naturally arises of the relationship between the Great Doubt and Dōgen's emphasis on pre-reflective without-thinking. First, let us consider one of the most difficult *practical* problems one encounters in the quest for without-thinking. When actually in that mode of awareness, one cannot be reflectively self-conscious of that fact. Insofar as knowing is a thinking act, one can only know when one is *not* in the mode of without-thinking. As we will see, one of the major functions of the Zen Master is to give the student information regarding the state of his or her consciousness; the ultimate aim is to help the student enter into without-thinking. To effect this state, the student is frozen into a state of not-thinking—a nonconceptual, nondiscriminating consciousness. Although experiencing does not itself cease, the intellectual sifting of that experience is no longer attempted and the person is not functioning or active at all. Presumably, everything blurs into a monistic whole. Judging from Hakuin's metaphors of the great expanse of ice and the person frozen at the edge of the precipice, this locked-in state of nonconceptual awareness is what he calls the Great Doubt.

The Great Doubt can also be seen in the spiritual quest described in Chapter 5, where the initial steps taken by the Zen disciple arise from a feeling of dissatisfaction with ordinary experience. The core of that dissatisfaction is a rejection of the retrospective reconstruction of reality. In other words, the Zen disciple finds that conceptual categories never quite contain the richness of experience—and the more one tries to express adequately what one feels, the more dissatisfied one becomes. Concepts filter experience; they are abstractions that become objectified as needs, desires, and fears. Aware that one has been conditioned to experience in certain prescribed ways, the novice no longer knows how to encounter things simply as they are. The Great Doubt is the crystallization of this view.

Before the student's training, his or her dissatisfaction is based on vague intuitions about the shortcomings of ordinary experience. But after years of Zen discipline, the difference between the reconstruction of experience and the direct experience of things has been experientially verified. Yet this understanding in itself does not resolve the problem but rather intensifies it. Aware that one must overcome the tendency to filter experience through previously learned categories, the student finds this impossible. In fact, the more effort exerted in trying to break down thinking, the more deeply one is entrapped in nihilistic not-thinking. Authentic without-thinking seems always to elude one's grasp.

All efforts being rejected and even ridiculed by the Zen Master, a state of deep depression may set in. The disciple may feel like quitting, but much has already been sacrificed: name, family identity, social class, possessions, and years of arduous discipline. Although one may feel no progress has been made in one's practice, to leave the monastery now is to be no one, a being without identity. Thus, the Zen novice is at an impasse: the secular identity no longer exists; the religious identity is still inchoate. On all sides the student is engulfed by nothingness. This is a dark nothingness, the nothingness of complete nihilation, the nothingness of not-thinking rather than without-thinking. Aware that one must not be bound to conceptual thinking, the student merely negates all thought, unable to find the standpoint which neither affirms nor denies. With no other alternative, the student returns to the practice. No longer sitting to be enlightened, one merely sits to sit. Feeling almost dead in any case, no longer protecting any part of the self, the disciple sits with abandonment, totally unconcerned with the consequences. At this point, the Great Doubt may arise: a still-point of terrible tension in which one gives oneself up to the feeling of nowhere to go. This is Hakuin's great expanse of ice.

The Great Doubt is not enlightenment, however; it is a stage to be surpassed by the Great Death. Achieved through a negative route, the Great Doubt is a not-thinking that has been restricted until there is nothing left for it to deny. Authentic without-thinking, on the other hand, is the source of thinking and not-thinking; it is prior to them and can never be achieved through thinking or not-thinking. In other words, from Hakuin's perspective, realization cannot be achieved by means of a gradual process. It is a leap. This is why he places such emphasis on the Great Death as a sudden awakening—the arising of a completely new standpoint outside the not-thinking of the Great Doubt.

Let us now investigate the nature of the Great Death in more detail. Zen Master Shibayama writes:

A Japanese Zen Master in the Tokugawa period named Shido Bunan had a *waka* poem:

Die while alive, and be completely dead,
then do whatever you will, all is good.

The aim of Zen training is to die while alive, that is, to actually become the self of no-mind, and no-form, and then to revive as the True Self of no-mind and no-form. In Zen training, therefore, what is most important is for one to revive from the abyss of unconsciousness. Zen training is *not* the emotional process of just being in the state of oneness, nor is it just to have the "feeling" of no-mind. *Prajna* wisdom (true wisdom) has to shine out after breaking through the extremity of the Great Doubt, and then still further training is needed so that one can freely live the Zen life and work in the world as a new man.[17]

The distinctions made by Shibayama in this short passage are significant. To experience the Great Death, one must revive from the monistic nondifferentiation of the Great Doubt, that frozen state of negation Hakuin called the great expanse of ice. To die to that empty monism is to be born to presence. Recall Hakuin's experience wherein the sound of the temple bell precipitated his realization. In Dōgen's life, we may remember, it was Nyojō's chastising of a monk for falling asleep that performed the same function. Other masters have experienced the awakening of the Great Death at the sight of a peach blossom or at the sound of bamboo striking a rock. All these experiences involve a direct apprehension of the sensed stimulus, an acceptance that completely fills the individual's consciousness. This description is reminiscent of Dōgen's analyses, and perhaps we can best focus on the meaning of the Great Death by considering its relationship to Dōgen's *genjōkōan*.

When frozen within the Great Doubt, Hakuin heard the voice of the Zen Master as if it were coming from afar. In other words, his primary experience was that of the empty stillness metaphorically expressed as the great expanse of ice. Yet, objectively speaking, there was no stillness in things as they were; it was merely a projection of Hakuin's state of mind. There was thus a conflict between the phenomenon Hakuin was directly experiencing (the voice) and the consciousness of the icy void projected over it. Clearly, this was not a state of *genjōkōan*, the direct presence of things as they are. The sheet of ice was a delusion clouding the flux of *uji* ("being-time"). When the temple bell struck, however, and the sound "smashed through the ice," Hakuin became nothing other than the experience of hearing-the-sound-of-the-bell. This was pure presence, the directly experienced *genjōkōan*, the state of without-thinking.

In other words, frozen in not-thinking, Hakuin's Great Doubt did not allow any conceptualization to enter consciousness; but this was unsatisfactory. To detach oneself willfully from all thinking, one has to *objectify* one's own thought processes, and in so doing one takes an intentional attitude toward thought. This means that one has also objectified one's self—one has not yet experienced the Great Death of the ego. When that last residual sense of the self is finally abandoned, however, one no longer takes any intentional standpoint at all. As pure without-thinking, one's formerly empty consciousness is suddenly filled by the simple sounding-of-the-bell. There is no I and no bell but rather the hearing of the bell: the apprehending of perfect *genjōkōan*. This is the pure state of without-thinking. But Hakuin still erred, of course. As soon as he had his pure, without-thinking experience, he reflected on it egocentrically, seeing it as unparalleled. Thus, the moment of without-thinking passed away as Hakuin started to think about it. It would take Master Shōju to bring Hakuin to the realization that enlightenment is not a moment but a continuous process.

Let us try to describe more precisely Hakuin's experience in Dōgen's terms. Both Hakuin's delusory expanse of ice and his later hearing-of-the-bell emerge out of their respective occasions (*jisetsu*). Both experiential events are based on the presence of things as they are; even a delusion does not arise *ex nihilo*. Dōgen maintains that presence is always, in all circumstances, immediately available to us. Enlightenment is always there to be authenticated.

Nevertheless, there is still a difference between Hakuin's two experiences. The frozen monism was present only insofar as Hakuin was resolute in cutting off all thoughts. It would have been inauthentic for Hakuin to deny what he was experiencing. Yet the icy stillness was part of the occasion only because Hakuin's consciousness posited it. Certainly, Hakuin was aware of this even though he may have been in no state to analyze it. Through Hakuin's own determination to live through his own experience unanalytically, however bizarre it might become, and through the skill of his master in forcing him beyond the point of no return, the flow of his reflective consciousness froze. His self-delusion that he could pursue and achieve a goalless goal was rigidly crystallized in front of him. Insofar as Hakuin had not yet accepted himself as nothingness, he brought something into the situation. Only when he let go, only when he fully let the presence be as it is without addition, did he achieve full authentication. It happened briefly at hearing the temple bell, but the basic reorientation of his character really began with his being struck unconscious with the broomstick. Only when Hakuin disappeared did he fully achieve his personhood.

## ZEN TACTICS

All the techniques discussed here aim at intensifying the Great Doubt within the student. For, as we have seen, Hakuin maintained that once the Great Doubt had arisen, the disciple will eventually experience an insight proportional to the intensity of the doubt.

Especially in the modern Rinzai tradition, the Zen Master focuses his training techniques not on enlightenment itself but on the penultimate stage: the Great Doubt. The theory is that if the Great Doubt becomes sufficiently crystallized, the Great Death (enlightenment) will spontaneously follow at some point.

One of the primary purposes of these techniques is to give the disciple information about the state of his or her consciousness. Since without-thinking is prereflective, one can easily deceive oneself as to the purity of one's consciousness. The techniques mentioned here are used to show students in a direct and unequivocal way that they are *not* in the nonconceptualizing state of without-thinking. The Zen Master accomplishes this goal by rejecting manifestations of thinking or not-thinking or by creating a situation in which a without-thinking response is abruptly produced—thereby manifesting the qualitative difference between this new state and what the disciple had *thought* was without-thinking. Let us consider an example of each sort.

In the first strategy, the Zen Master devises an intellectual "double-bind"[18] situation; that is, the disciple is placed in a predicament where one can neither affirm nor deny, at least in any intellectual manner. In the following example, the double bind is patent:

> Master Shuzan [Ch: Shou-shan] held up his staff, and showing it to the assembled disciples said, "You monks, if you call this a staff, you are committed to the name. If you call it not-a-staff, you negate the fact. Tell me, monks, what do you call it?"[19]

On a more fundamental level, however, the double bind is illusory. From Shuzan's standpoint, there is really no conflict at all; he is calling for a without-thinking response, one that takes no positing stance whatsoever. In other words, Shuzan is trying to intensify the Great Doubt in his students by closing off their usual avenues of response (thinking and not-thinking). Because the Zen Master is aware of the prereflective standpoint (and in fact exemplifies it) in posing the question, the situation differs from the double-bind situation described by Bateson; that is, the Zen position explicitly recognizes *three* modes of response (affirmation, negation, neutrality), only two of which have been closed off. From the viewpoint of the confused and frustrated Zen student, though, the two situations might appear comparable. That is, accustomed to resolving problems with reflective analysis, the student may believe that the master is demanding the impossible. As Mumon tells us in his commentary, however, there *are* other alternatives: "Kisei [Ch: Kuei-shêng] lost no time in snatching the staff, and throwing it on the ground he demanded in return, 'What is this?' "[20] Kisei eluded Shuzan's conceptual trap by a spontaneous act which did not allow the master's question to create a double bind.

As for the second strategy, eliciting a without-thinking response and calling the student's attention to it, we have the following story:

> A young man came to the Zen Master Gensha [Ch: Hsüan-sha] and asked, "I have come over here seeking the Truth. Where can I start to get into Zen?" At this Gensha asked, "Can you hear the murmuring of the mountain stream?" "Yes, I can hear it." "Enter Zen from there!"[21]

Gensha's point was not that the student should dive into the brook, but that he should relinquish intellectual questions and enter into the immediacy of his own experience, as exemplified by the direct way he hears the murmuring of the brook. Here we see the master precipitating a momentary state of without-thinking for use as a comparison with the student's previous state of thinking or not-thinking. Let us now turn directly to the techniques themselves.

## Koan Practice

Many Zen Masters, especially those of the Rinzai tradition, make koan practice the focal point of training disciples. This does not mean that the koan replaces zazen, but rather that it becomes the focus of concentration within zazen. Without objectifying the koan, the student tries to *become* the koan itself. Let us take as our example Jōshū's "*Mu!*", which Hakuin himself studied and often used in teaching. He advises one to concentrate on the koan as follows:

> The area below my navel down to my loins and the soles of my feet is all Chao-chou's *Mu*. What principles can this *Mu* possibly have! The area below my navel down to my loins and the soles of my feet is all my original face. Where can there be nostrils in this original face![22]

Hakuin refers to this method of introspection as *naikan*, a practice not limited to seated meditation. As part of one's waking consciousness, it is the nucleus around which the Great Doubt coalesces. Within this koan practice, the bifurcation between body and mind dissolves. The significance of the *Mu* koan is neither a concept nor something physical. Rather, it is the very *source* of the person, the prereflective without-thinking out of which all experiences and differentiations arise. Consequently, to be fully practicing *Mu* (the koan) is to enter into consciousness of *mu*. This is the state of no-mind *(mushin)*.

Furthermore, in a comprehensive practice the koan also serves as the foundation for the dynamic interaction between disciple and master. If the student were merely instructed to *become* the koan, one might fall into objectifying and thinking *about* the koan. To avoid this, interviews with the Zen Master called *sanzen* or *dokusan* are required. In the middle of an extended period of meditation, the student is called to the Zen Master's room. Though its opening and closing are ritualistic, the actual interview can be remarkably free in form. Before going to the *sanzen* room, the disciple rings a bell twice. A Zen Master can often determine the student's state of mind merely from the sound of the bell or the footsteps approaching the room.

After entering the room and making the appropriate (very formal and rather drawn out) bows, the student begins a dialogue with the master. Many of the famous Zen dialogues *(mondō)* are derived from accounts of these exchanges. When Hakuin presented Shōju with a verse expressing his understanding, Shōju asked him about the nature of Jōshū's *"Mu!"* and, dissatisfied with the response, grasped him by the nose. Since both the Zen Master and, ideally, the student are in a state of without-thinking (both have been doing zazen immediately before the interview), and since without-thinking need not observe rules or formalities, there are really no restrictions on either participant. The student may even defy the master's initial response with a counterassault, as did Hakuin.

An important point to remember, however, is that statements in *sanzen* are authentic or inauthentic not in reference to the proposition spoken but in reference to the speaker's state of mind. What is judged is the quality of the state of without-thinking, the source of the utterance, not the truth of the proposition or the content of the statement. Consider, for example, the following story about the Chinese Zen Master Hōgen (Ch: Fa-yen). To the question "What is Buddha?" one of the disciples responded *"Hei-tei-doji Rai-gu-ka"* ("the deity of fire seeks fire"). Hōgen rebuked the disciple for this reply, calling him a fake. Offended, the monk started to leave the monastery. But a Zen Master of Hōgen's reputation must have had a reason for such a strong reaction, so the monk returned to Hōgen, putting to him the question: "What is Buddha?" Without hesitation, he replied, *"Hei-tei-doji Rai-gu-ka!"* The monk was suddenly enlightened.[23]

The crux of the story is that although the literal statement remained the same, the quality of consciousness making the utterance was different. The student's response had been conceptually filtered and premeditated, however subtly—it rose out of thinking. But Hōgen's response was spontaneous and prereflective, rising out of without-thinking. With this contrast manifested right before his eyes, the student was enlightened. In other words, the Zen Master is not interested *in* what the student has to say; rather, he observes what one reveals *by* what one says or does.[24] Through his own practice and realization, the Zen Master can distinguish between genuinely spontaneous without-thinking and mediated forgery. Since the master is without-thinking, the student cannot predict what the master might do or ask. Therefore, one must be completely responsive to whatever might happen. Any tinge of premeditated or conceptually oriented behavior will be discerned and rebuked by the master.

The koan thus intensifies the Great Doubt in three general ways. First, it concentrates zazen practice by breaking down the conceptual distinction between body and mind. The *whole* person, body-and-mind, becomes Jōshū's *"Mu!"* Second, since it is basically paradoxical, the koan itself is not resolvable by either thinking or not-thinking. The search for another approach, when supplemented with the *naikan* form of zazen, leads to the discovery of without-thinking. Third, in *sanzen* the master himself exemplifies without-thinking and chastises all actions of the student not arising from without-thinking.

## Striking

Striking may be used in various ways, but the underlying purpose is usually the same: a summons to abandon thought and return to without-thinking. Hence, monks in the meditation hall who are dozing off or lost in fantasies may be struck with a long, flat stick to bring them back to direct awareness. The crisp, biting sting of the stick is so sharp that there is no place for reflections to enter, at least for the moment. In this way, the sting (as well as the abrupt "crack!" resounding through the hall) propels the meditator into without-thinking. By the very fact that one experiences that return, one immediately recognizes the state of consciousness prior to the striking to have been different. Thus, the striking not only restores without-thinking; it also makes the meditator aware of the contrast between without-thinking and daydreaming or sleeping. This awareness may either intensify the Great Doubt or help the meditator authenticate what he or she is, right then and there. Shōju's beatings exacerbated Hakuin's despair all the more, for example, but the householder's beating with the broomstick triggered his insight.

Striking can also be used in the formal or informal interrelations between master and disciple. In this case, there is again a test of the student's spontaneous responsiveness. By striking the student abruptly, the master proves the student's mind to have been somewhere else. In other words, by catching the disciple off guard, he verifies that the student was thinking about what just happened or what will happen next—instead of being centered in the koan or genjōkōan. Sometimes the student may attempt to strike the master (there are no fixed rules once sanzen begins), but the master would know if this attempt were premeditated or emotional rather than spontaneous.*

## Shouting

Shouting is another technique used to intensify the Great Doubt. After Rinzai spoke on the nature of the true person of no status,

---

*In this respect, we see a point of similarity between Zen and the martial arts. Both emphasize responsiveness rather than premeditated or emotional reaction.

we recall, a monk stood to ask what the true person really is. Immediately Rinzai stepped down, grabbed the monk, and shouted, "Speak! Speak!" The shout, like striking, can be used to stun or shock the student, cutting off reflection and propelling one into momentary without-thinking. In this way, a shout may serve the same purpose as the stick in the meditation hall.

Furthermore, a spontaneous shout is itself a full expression of one's being, unifying the body and mind and leaving no room for self-reflection.* It can thus be considered an abrupt form of chant. In Zen, the chant is used as a meditative exercise in which the ego is immersed in the sounds of the words being chanted. Just as the chanter *becomes* the chant and loses all sense of agency, the shouter (for a moment at least) *becomes* the shout.

Both shouting and striking exemplify without-thinking. Moreover, by their abrupt spontaneity, they instill a temporary state of without-thinking in the student as well. This experience may reveal to the disciple that the previous state of mind had not been pure. Through such reminders, the Zen disciple is forced to reject all conceptualization as soon as it arises. This objectification of conceptual thinking (so that it can be rejected) is the basis of the Great Doubt. When the Great Doubt has fully coalesced, a point of terrible tension arises. Inevitably, the tension breaks and the radically new perspective of the Great Death arises. From that point on, the Zen monk will function effectively, without thinking.

## DŌGEN ZEN AND HAKUIN ZEN

Although the Sōtō and Rinzai orders are distinct, we have not found any intrinsic philosophical disagreement between Dōgen, the supposed founder of the Japanese Sōtō tradition, and Hakuin, the most prominent Japanese Rinzai Master. That is to say, Hakuin's Great Doubt and Great Death are not necessarily incompatible with the basic categories of Dōgen's phenomenology: thinking, not-thinking, and without-thinking. Certainly, Hakuin criticizes silent-

---

*Again, the shout is also utilized in martial arts as a way of unifying body and mind so that the participant is fully focused on his or her present action.

illumination zazen but, as we have seen, Dōgen's conception of zazen is precisely as an authenticating activity filling one's daily life. Conversely, Dōgen is critical of koan study when it is a distraction from the immediate self-authentication available in zazen, yet Hakuin's emphasis on meditation in daily activity also goes beyond any fixation on technique, to an immersion in the Great Doubt, which must be maintained at all times in all places. Thus, Dōgen's *genjōkōan*—the presence of things as they are—is an appropriate complement to Hakuin's *dōchū no kufū*, "[meditative] diligence in the midst of activity."

The two masters are distinguishable on many points, however. Dōgen's focus is on direct authentication while Hakuin's is on the Great Doubt; Dōgen resists the idea of stages of development while Hakuin speaks not only of stages on the way to enlightenment but of stages *within* enlightenment; Dōgen encourages an earnest self-questioning in his disciples while Hakuin feels the master must provoke that questioning. Such differences are critical in the structuring of practical training techniques, but when we consider the Zen Buddhist understanding of the person per se, we note an underlying similarity in Dōgen and Hakuin. Both masters emphasize, for example, the importance of personal quest—that is, both urge that we seek an answer to the question "What am I?" This question, however, does not have an answer, at least not one that can be expressed discursively. The question is resolved only when one returns to the source of the experiencing process, when one lets go of preconceived notions of the self. This is Dōgen's molting of body-mind and Hakuin's Great Death. There seems to be some disagreement as to whether we should think of this letting go as a single capping experience of a long process, as in Hakuin, or as an inner dynamic of the process itself, as in Dōgen. Part of this disagreement is semantic, however. In both accounts, the enlightenment experience is all-encompassing and holistic, yet continuously renewed in all of one's daily activities.

In Part II we have traced the spiritual development of the person within the Zen context and have seen why our philosophical attempt to understand Zen must always be qualitatively different from actually practicing Zen. Certainly, many of us have followed a line of thought to its end and perhaps had a glimpse of the chasm of relativity and negative emptiness. Yet we also have had the luxury of being able to retreat from that point. Unlike the Zen monk, we have not burned all our bridges. With our culturally instilled sense of a personal, individual essence, we can but vaguely imagine what it is like for the Japanese monk to cut himself off from the social context that once defined his very personhood; we can but vaguely understand the experience of being locked into the Great Doubt. To compare without-thinking arising within the Great Death to the momentary prereflective consciousness of a baseball player or a medic responding to a call for help is rather like comparing an artist's utter involvement with his or her work to my doodling on an old newspaper while talking on the telephone. In coming to understand the nature of the Zen person, we have also seen how *unlike* us he or she is.

To conclude this discussion of Zen training, let us turn again to Bashō and a story from his own training days. His Zen teacher, Butchō, had criticized him for writing poetry instead of practicing the Zen disciplines. Bashō responded that poetry is "simply what is happening right here, right now." Bashō believed his haiku were expressive of the Zen spirit: they accept the present moment without trying to evaluate it or preserve it as a symbol of anything other than what it is. A haiku is not an aesthetic object to be admired by posterity; it is a way of expressing an event of *genjō-kōan*—a glimpse of the poet present in the moment the poem was written. Demonstrating his point, Bashō wrote the following:

| | |
|---|---|
| *Michinobe no* | A roadside Rose of Sharon. |
| *Mikuge wa uma ni* | By a horse, |
| *Kuwarekeri*[25] | Eaten. |

After hearing this poem, Butchō was satisfied that Bashō was not wasting his time writing haiku.

# Part III
## THE PERSON AS ACT

# CHAPTER 9

# Zen Action/Zen Person

Zen Buddhism's view of the person cannot be directly analyzed in philosophical terms. If one were to ask whether Zen postulates an essence to the person, we would have to reply that it neither affirms nor denies this view. To affirm or deny the existence of such an essence would be to operate within the realm of thinking. Yet Zen Buddhism would also claim that adopting this neutral attitude as a philosophical standpoint would also be unacceptable, since to refuse to consider the whole question and to hold that no categories whatsoever apply to the person is to fall into the nihilism of not-thinking.

Zen maintains the perspective of without-thinking. That is to say, it achieves a standpoint prior to either arguing or not arguing the existence of an essence to the person. In this regard, the master lets the context determine his characterization. Part of that context is the questioner's state of mind, and the master replies to the *student's* question rather than the student's *question*. If a student reveals a nihilistic attitude, the master might say there is an essence to the person. If the student is bound to categories, the master might say there is no essence to the person. In this way, the master can more powerfully enter into the self-constituting of the student's own experiential flow. By seeing the student's perspective, the master can modify that perspective as needed. Thus, the Zen Buddhist strives to return to the point at which experience, including thought, initially occurs. This emphasis on without-thinking is what is distinctive in the Zen understanding of the person. Although there are Western philosophers, particularly in the French existentialist tradition, who recognize the uniqueness of prereflective experience, in Zen Buddhism alone is this mode of consciousness the central focus of a spiritual way of life.

## NOTHINGNESS AND WITHOUT-THINKING

In Japanese culture a person is primarily defined *relationally*; that is, one's social situation determines who one is as a person. Without an overarching framework to establish relationships between self and others or self and things, the person has no specificity, no distinctive meaning. While Westerners often believe that as individuals we determine or at least take part in our relationships (with others, with nature, with objects), the Japanese typically believe that relationships precede any determination of the person; there is nothing external which can take part in the relationship. To understand the nature of the person within Zen Buddhism, therefore, the context and the relationships arising out of it are of primary importance.

As we have seen, the Zen context of the person is *mu* or "nothingness." *Mu* establishes the relationships through which the Zen disciple achieves personal meaning, the most basic relationship being that of without-thinking. At first, it may seem odd to regard without-thinking as a *relationship*. Our natural inclination is to consider it an attitude of the Zen Buddhist or perhaps an activity which he or she performs. From the Zen perspective, though, to conceive of without-thinking in this way is to put the cart before the horse. Without-thinking is prior to the person; it forms that out of which the Zen Buddhist achieves authentic personhood. Along the same lines, it is also misleading to interpret without-thinking as a necessary (and perhaps sufficient) condition for personhood. To conceive of without-thinking as a condition reifies it in such a way as to lose its double-ended relational character. We must remember that it is out of without-thinking that the two related components are defined; without-thinking is the source of not only the Zen Buddhist's meaning but also the meaning of that with which he or she is associated at the time. If a Zen Buddhist examines a flower, both the person and the flower become meaningful through the relationship of without-thinking.

It might be helpful to translate this notion into a schematic rendering which compares it to Japanese secular relationships. Although generalized, Figures 1 and 2 emphasize how without-thinking defines the Zen person in a way radically different from the way a person is defined secularly in Japan.

Figure 1. Mr. A in Three Secular Contexts

Context: economic
Relationship: occupational hierarchy
Situation: two members of a corporation at gift-giving time (e.g., New Year)

Boss
B

Employee
A

Persons A and B defined by relationship as "employee" and "boss"

Context: commercial
Relationship: mercantile indebtedness
Situation: business transaction in a shop

Customer
A

Salesperson
B

Persons A and B defined by relationship as "customer" and "salesperson"

Context: familial
Relationship: age hierarchy
Situation: discussion between members of family

Father
B

Son
A

Persons A and B defined by relationship as "son" and "father"

Again we must restrain our Western tendency to regard Mr. A as a person going from one context to the next, from one situation to another. In the Japanese secular framework, Mr. A is only a person insofar as he is *in* these contexts. If we could list all the relational determinations (employee, customer, son, and so on), we would not have a list of roles that Mr. A plays—we would have what Mr. A is *as a person*. Without these associations Mr. A would be a solitary chess piece with neither a chessboard nor a rulebook to give him function and significance. Though ontically distinct, he would still lack distinctive meaning.

Moreover—and this will be a significant point later in our discussion—Mr. A understands himself as a person within the same categories as others understand him. Although he may have private feelings, his meaning *as a person* is predominantly public and objectively observable. His discharge of moral responsibilities, his use of language (formal/informal, humble/honorific), even his usage of leisure time are all aspects of his personhood and, as such, are generally circumscribed by his publicly visible associations. In other words, for Mr. A to function as a person *(ningen)*, he must see himself as functioning in certain preestablished relationships. He cannot act without this presuppositional understanding of who he is in that context. If we were to ask both Mr. A and an uninvolved observer why he used a certain honorific language form in a certain conversation, we would probably receive the same reply: that he is speaking to his employer, or to a customer, or whomever. In the Zen Buddhist context, this is not the case. Figure 2 depicts that context.

In the context of *mu*, there is a crucial difference between the Zen Buddhist's experience and an outside observer's characterization of it. In secular contexts, both the experiencing person and the observer are dependent on various categories. Both are bound by their common dependence on thinking. In Zen situations, however, personhood is grounded in without-thinking rather than thinking. So there is necessarily a gap between the Zen Buddhist's own without-thinking experience of relationships and an outside observer's objectified, thinking characterization of them. This gap correlates to the one between a prereflective experience and one's own

Figure 2. Mr. *A* in the Zen Context

Context: *mu* ("nothingness")
Relationship: without-thinking
Situation: (self)–(other) or (subject)–(object) or (speaker)–(language) or (artist)–
    (artwork)

|         |           |
|---------|-----------|
| *A*     | *B*       |
| (self)  | (other)   |
| (subject) | (object) |
| (speaker) | (language) |
| (artist) | (artwork) |

The double arrow represents the without-thinking relationship between the Zen person *(A)* and the thing being experienced *(B)*. Note that *B* need not be a person.
Ellipses indicate the nonobjectifying standpoint of without-thinking as experienced
*within* the context of *mu*. Parentheses enclose terms which an observer *outside* the
context might use to characterize the situation.

retrospective reconstruction of that experience. That is to say, in
reflectively characterizing an experience no longer present, one
must resort to an objectified, thinking account.

On the other hand, the schematic representation of without-
thinking in Figure 2, with its empty ellipses, may seem nihilistic; it
appears to nullify all possibilities for the person to have any specific meaning. That is, if the Zen person achieves meaning through
relational functions, and if those functions are all grounded in the
nonobjectifying mode of without-thinking, does this imply that the
Zen person's experience is totally empty and lacking in all determinateness? Obviously, this cannot be the case, since we have seen
that the Zen Buddhist is in direct and specific relationship with the
thing being experienced at that moment. The Zen Master's without-
thinking relationship with his student, for example, has a different
content from his relationship with his teacup, even though the
*mode* of relating is the same in both cases.

Here there is a similarity to our Taoist allegory of the bell. As
we recall, the Taoist view of Nonbeing is both indeterminate and
determinate. In itself, Nonbeing is completely ineffable and uncontradictable, but it is also nonfunctional. When specified by
Being (as the casting of the bell specifies the space-within-the-bell),

however, it is determinate and *functional*. Similarly, if we try to characterize the Zen Buddhist per se, he or she is without determinateness. This is the Zen version of *anātman* or no-ego *(muga)*.

Yet, taken at any given moment, the Zen person is fully operative *relationally*. In other words, the Zen person's activity is at all times meaningful though we cannot express the meaning without considering that to which he or she is related in a without-thinking way. In Chapter 4, this aspect of the person within the context of nothingness was expressed in terms of the equivalence between no-mind *(mushin)* and functional mind *(yōshin*; Ch: *yung-hsin)*. Insofar as one is functional—that is, related to something—the Zen Buddhist has a specific meaning objectifiable by the thought of an external observer or by one's own subsequent retrospective analysis. Within the functionality itself, however, there is merely relatedness. This is the contrast with the secular person: while the secular person must have a presupposed status in order to act, the Zen Buddhist is, in Rinzai's words, a person of no status or nothingness-status. That is, the Zen ideal is to act spontaneously in the situation without first objectifying it in order to define one's role. The Zen person is an operative part of the situation but is not, strictly speaking, defined by it.

Again, the Zen Buddhist does not have a different meaning in each situation any more than our secular Mr. A has many different roles. In both secular Japan and Zen Buddhism, the person is not something that *has* meaning or *has* relationships; rather, one achieves meaning *through* relationships. To this extent at least, Zen is still characteristically Japanese, but that does not mean Japanese Zen Buddhism is strictly culture-bound. Zen's image of the person is formulated, not surprisingly, in response to the secular image of the person within his or her own culture. That is why Zen insists on returning to the origin of personhood. That origin is the relationship from which one derives meaning—namely, without-thinking. Unlike the secular person whose thinking and not-thinking relationships are numerous and ever-changing, the Zen person is grounded only in without-thinking, since this alone arises out of the *mu* embracing all Zen activity. One is not thereby limited in the range or variety of experience, however. Although the relationship remains the same, *A* and *B* can be quite different depending on the situation. This is one reason why Zen has influenced so many aspects of Japanese culture. Advocating a mode of relating rather than a set of doctrines, its applicability is virtually limitless. Without-thinking can be the operative relationship between artist and artwork, master and disciple, swordsman and sword, speaker and language. To gain a clear picture of how without-thinking manifests itself in these various situations, let us turn now to a final example.

## WITHOUT-THINKING AND LANGUAGE

At first, this topic might seem to present insurmountable difficulties to our assertion that without-thinking is a prerequisite for the Zen life. Although verbal utterances such as shouting and the paradoxical koan are representative techniques based in without-thinking, clearly the Zen Master cannot limit his speaking to such speech acts alone. How does the master's without-thinking display itself in instructing a new student in the correct placement of the hands during zazen, for example, or in ordering a monk to prepare the fire for the bath? In practical intercourse with the unenlightened, it would seem the master has to abandon his nonconceptualizing standpoint in order to share in the same conceptual framework as his listeners. This is not as problematic as it might seem, however.

First, we ask whether the enlightened person should speak at all: does silence present a way of avoiding this whole issue? No. To *choose* silence is to fall victim to the nihilism of not-thinking. The Zen Buddhist achieves meaning through his or her relatedness, and complete silence is not a satisfactory mode of relating. On the other hand, to relate to people and things through the dependence on conceptualized presuppositions (thinking) is also clearly inappropriate. The Chinese Taoist, Chuang Tzŭ, notes the same predicament:

> If you talk in a worthy manner, you can talk all day long and all of it will pertain to the Way. But if you talk in an unworthy manner, you can talk all day long and all of it will pertain to mere things. The

perfection of the Way and things—neither words nor silence are worthy of expressing it. Not to talk, not to be silent—this is the highest form of debate.[1]

What use of language is advocated here? How can the enlightened Zen person bring the without-thinking of the meditation hall into the secular discourse of the everyday world?

We must bear in mind that the master's original face—his primordial person, his true self—is not schizophrenically detached from the historical situation.[2] The Zen Master does not speak in tongues—he speaks Japanese. He does not cease to eat—he eats the same food as the other monks. He does not transcend the world— he is firmly implanted in it. The Zen Master does not *undo* his conditionality; rather, he understands its nature and its limits. As already noted, to an outside observer a Zen Master seems to be working within many of the same categories as unenlightened people. He knows how to chop wood efficiently, how to plant a garden, how to prepare food. A common expression is that the enlightened person appears "extraordinarily ordinary."

Yet, as we have also seen, no two Zen Masters are alike. Each has his own teaching methods and own manner of expressing his insight. We have already remarked on the difference between Dōgen's basically phenomenological approach and Hakuin's fundamentally aesthetic and psychologistic tendencies. A Zen Master is like the rest of us in that certain words rather than others will occur to him and he will display a specific gestalt developed in previous experience. Yet he differs from unenlightened persons in his perspective on his conceptual conditioning. Rather than altering the nature of his prereflective experience by perpetually restructuring it into conceptual categories, the Zen Master's concepts arise *in response* to his basic without-thinking approach. This difference is exemplified in the relationship between master and student in *sanzen.*

When the student confronts the master in *sanzen*, the master does not immediately filter his direct experience of the student's personhood. Sitting before the master, students are allowed to manifest themselves just as they are. Without thinking in terms of student or master, novice or adept, the Zen Master merely *"lets be"* this encounter in its prereflective form. The student's behavior will subsequently activate some response from the master. That is, once the student has presented himself or herself to the master, the master will do what the situation evokes—whether that be encouragement, straightforward instructions, or a slap in the face. In this regard, he may take into consideration the student's previous efforts, but the next time the student comes for *sanzen*, the procedure is repeated. Again the master faces the personhood of the student as if he has met him or her for the first time. *Each time is a first time.*[3] Like us, the Zen Master is influenced by his circumstances; but unlike us, he is influenced not by the past but by the present situation. This statement requires further explication.

Because of his previous experiences, a Zen Master is inevitably *conditioned*. The typical Japanese Zen Master cannot, for example, respond to his student in Arabic rather than Japanese. In this regard, the Zen Master is no different from an unenlightened person. Yet this does not mean that the Zen Master is *determined* to speak in Japanese. He might, for example, respond by slapping the student in the face without uttering a word. From the Zen Master's perspective, the conditions of the past merely present alternative possibilities for action in the present.

On the other hand, we should not fall victim to the opposite extreme of viewing the master's actions as merely arbitrary: the master's without-thinking response is an action determined by the situation of the present. What the student presents in *sanzen* determines how the master will respond, within the possibilities open to him by his conditions. His activity arises out of the immediate relationship to the presence of what is there at the moment. How is this act distinguishable from the determined behavior of the unenlightened thinking person? Put succinctly, the thinking person allows previous conditioning to determine what he or she experiences in the present. If one's linguistic training allows one to recognize five kinds of snow, for example, one will mistakenly believe one only *experiences* five kinds of snow. Indeed, the thinking person may even claim that in reality there are exactly five kinds of snow. Such a person has cut himself off from his own prereflective experience;

prereflectively, each snowflake is neither the same nor different from others—there is merely the experiencing of the snow as it is now. If the thinking person were more mindful of this, he or she would realize the limitations of linguistic distinctions. But in ignoring such experiences, one becomes more and more bound to previously learned concepts, thereby becoming more and more determined by one's past.

In Zen, language is evoked by the present occasion itself; it is not merely a mapping of the present in terms of learned structures. In this respect language has more of a poetic than a discursive dimension. Heidegger writes:

> Poetry proper [for Heidegger, the purest form of speaking] is never merely a higher mode *(melos)* of everyday language. It is rather the reverse: everyday language is a forgotten and therefore used-up poem, from which there hardly resounds a call any longer.[4]

From this standpoint, in ordinary experience one immediately colors the purity of one's prereflective experience by imposing categories on it without confirming their appropriateness in the particular instance. If a teacher, for example, allows the category of *student* to filter what she hears from the person presently standing before her, she immediately loses her openness to the situation and is prepared to respond only to certain types of behavior. It is different for the Zen Master who remains within the relationship of without-thinking until an appropriate thought arises out of that experience. I once heard someone ask a Buddhist monk if he tired of continually answering the same questions from students. The monk replied that he had never heard the same question twice—each time the question was asked, it was asked by a different person. Heidegger also speaks of thoughts arising of themselves rather than as the object of conscious willing. In one of his poems he writes:

> We never come to thoughts. They come to us.
> That is the proper hour of discourse.
> Discourse cheers us to companionable reflection. Such reflection neither parades polemical opinions nor does it tolerate complaisant agreement. The sail of thinking keeps trimmed hard to the wind of the matter.

For such companionship a few perhaps may rise to be journeymen in
the craft of thinking. So that one of them, unforeseen, may become
a master.[5]

If the Zen Master were to allow concepts to distort his open encounter with students, he could not respond fully to the personhood
manifested by the students. Through his suppositionless without-
thinking, the Zen Master's response in sanzen reflects what the
student presents.

Upon hearing this account, we might still be tempted to ask,
"If the Zen Master is in the nonconceptualizing mode of without-
thinking, where do the words come from?" This is like the question
asked us by the mountain priest in the story related in Chapter 3.
After ringing the temple bell, we recall, he asked: "Now please
answer *my* question. Where did the sound of the bell come from
—from the metal casting or from the emptiness inside?"

How can we answer such a query? The sound of the mutual vi-
bration of *both* the casting and the air within it cannot be said to
have its origin in either; one cannot vibrate without the other. The
striker is the catalyst in the situation, but in itself it makes no contribution to the sound at all. Just so, there is no agency located
within the Zen Master. His original face is as empty as the hole
within the bell. Yet that original face is determinate and capable of
function because it has historical and physical *location*, the conditions comprising the present situation. The original face is not
dissolved into an ineffable absolute; it is living and breathing right
in front of us in the person of this Zen Master who may be seventy-
six years old, who speaks Japanese, and who has a wart on the side
of his nose. In terms of the analogy, the emptiness within is encased
by the historical situation. Therefore, without expectation, the present moment strikes the master and he responds with his whole
self—Being and Nonbeing, physical self and original face. The two
are not separate; they respond in unison. Whence does the present
situation originate? The master is not concerned with such questions. They are outside his verifiable experience and they inquire
into the nature of the thing-in-itself. The presence of the present
situation is the starting point from which the Zen Master acts.

Perhaps we can see now how we might have responded to the monk's unexpected question about the origin of the sound of the bell. We might have taken the loglike striker into our own hands and let the bell sound. The simple sound-of-the-bell-ringing-itself might have been accepted by the monk as an appropriate response, but only if the bell authentically rang itself—that is, only if there had been no premeditated, objectifying intention on our part.

Although it is easy to say "*let* the bell ring itself," in practice this is most difficult. For the bell to ring itself, we must bring nothing of our own to the ringing. If we can maintain this uninterfering posture *(wu-wei; makusa)*,[6] the bell will be struck with precisely the right force. To strike the bell too softly is to be attached to the form of the bell. The sound does not reside in the casting alone, just as the person is more than a set of historical conditions. On the other hand, to strike the bell too violently is to be nihilistic, to be attached to the formless. We cannot find the sound of the bell by breaking open the metal casting and liberating the void within, just as we cannot find our full sense of personhood by totally rejecting our historical conditions and seeking an ahistorical original face. For the bell to ring itself, there must be a harmonious unity between the Being and the Nonbeing of the bell. But how is this harmony achieved? It can only be achieved as a reflection of the personal harmony within the bell-ringer. Only if one is in a without-thinking relationship with the bell, only if one integrates the physical self and the original face, can one truly "let the bell ring itself."

In a similar way, the Zen Master does not speak, but, to use Heidegger's phrase, he lets "language itself speak."[7] For the enlightened, speaking is itself a response to the directly apprehended situation. Language should not predetermine experience; nor should it arise from an independent agent who brings something to the situation. Language must be the vibrating of the undetermined without-thinking within the conditions of the concrete occasion. Only if both aspects vibrate harmoniously does the language itself ring true. For the Zen Master, whether presenting his students with a koan or explaining the procedure for lighting the fire for the bath, insofar as his language is grounded in the relation of without-thinking and he is responsive to the situation presented to him, his language displays its own authenticity.

## ZEN ACTION/ZEN PERSON

The appropriateness of the title *Zen Action / Zen Person* is now evident. Because of the distinctive nature of without-thinking and the nothingness out of which it arises, the Zen person must always be considered as functioning relationally: outside of without-thinking, there is no person. From the Zen perspective, the person does not perform action; rather, action performs the person. In the words of Nishida: "It is not the case that there is an individual and then experience; rather, there is experience and then the individual."[8] Experience is constituted of its own accord; there is no consciously willed direction from a self standing outside it. If so, whence arises the delusory idea of the independent self?

Experience has a cumulative aspect. The possibilities of present responsiveness are circumscribed by the conditions derived from previous experience. When these conditions are conceptually categorized, they appear to constitute a self that determines the direction of activity. Yet the incompleteness of this image of the person gives rise to various problems. The more the person identifies with these conditions (the person as name, age, family relationship, educational background, and so on), the more one falls into the grasp of a deterministic view of behavior. In other words, if I direct my experience and am essentially such a list of conditions, then the direction of my experience is fundamentally nothing more than the determined effects of all those conditioned factors. Yet, insofar as no one is completely out of touch with his or her own prereflective experience, this conclusion does not reflect all of what one is. There is something more than mere determinacy from the past; there is also the present moment working in its own creative way. The more one is in touch with prereflective experience, the more certain one is that personhood is not simply reducible to a set of conceptual categories.

Yet there is a riddle lurking within this description. Prereflective experience is part of each individual's personhood. No one lacks

prereflective experience, yet some people are more grounded in the
mode of without-thinking than others. How can we account for this
discrepancy? It is critical that the "letting be" in without-thinking
be active, not passive. Consider the prereflective experience of
feeling-the-wind-on-one's-face. Even before this is objectified into
*face* and *wind*, it is already an experiential flow. Let us consider
what happens if we simply let this experience be. The direct experiencing will simply continue and, in fact, in certain situations
the word *wind* might even come to mind. This thought, arising
out of without-thinking, is as natural an occurrence in humans as
breathing or walking.

Experience, because of the cumulative effect of conditions acquired through past situations, *structures itself* through without-
thinking. Without-thinking is thus the source of thought, the source
of the person. On the other hand, prereflective experience can also
*be structured* through the analytic application of conceptual
categories. In this case, prereflective experience is reflectively
restructured by one's presuppositional concepts and this formulation may seem more authentic than the original experience. Thus, a
person may insist that one is an independent agent who performs
actions even though one's own prereflective experience reveals no
such agency. A consideration of without-thinking's role in art will
make this point clear.

It is a commonly accepted rule of artistic training that the student must first learn technique in order to transcend technique. To
learn technique is to be conditioned by cumulative experience to
perform certain acts in a certain way—the holding of a brush, the
fingering of a bamboo flute, the cutting of flowers. But to be conditioned by these rules only opens up possibilities of response. One
must overcome the danger of being *determined* by these rules, of
becoming so attached to these conditions acquired in the past that
the present is no longer creative. To transcend technique is to
respond to the presence of the moment now before us. The determinateness of past conditions must vibrate in unison with the openness of the present. A Taoist principle states that a painting should
be done in one stroke. In a literal sense, this is usually impossible,
but the point is that the painting must, in every instance, be one

act without the interference of conceptual reflection. Like making a single stroke with the brush, the painting of the picture must be an uninterrupted response to the present. Only then do the artist and the artwork ring true.

Thus, by being grounded in nonobjectifying without-thinking, the Zen Buddhist reveals personal presence just as it is. Through egoless responsiveness, the Zen Buddhist achieves freedom, creativity, compassion, and wisdom. One is *free* by not being determined solely by the past. One is *creative* by being responsive to the present moment expressing itself through one's own person. Through the relationship of without-thinking, both artist and artwork become distinctive. Each moment is new. Each time is a "first time." One is *compassionate* by being fully open to other people. Without presuppositions, one accepts them as they show themselves and one responds to what they present, not to what they are preconceived to be. One is *wise* by having the equanimity of without-thinking. Though conditioned by the past, one does not let the past conceal the openness of the present. One sees what-is as-it-is.

In concluding, we call yet again on the poet Bashō. In this haiku, he displays the Zen view of the continuity and the completeness of each moment of experience: there is no explanation for the apparent confusion of sensations, no attempt to capture a fleeting experience however exquisite. There is only the abiding in the presence of the moment as it is directly experienced:

| | |
|---|---|
| *Kane kiete* | The temple bell dies away |
| *Hana no ka wa tsuku* | But the fragrance of flowers resounds— |
| *Yūbe kana.*[9] | Evening. |

# CHAPTER 10

# Philosophical Postscript: Toward a Zen Humanism

In this final chapter we stand back from our analysis of the person in Japanese Zen Buddhism in order to investigate its relevance to issues of present concern in the West. In the past century, the Western view of the person has been influenced by a number of developments both within philosophy and without. The theory of evolutionary continuity between homo sapiens and other animal species, psychoanalytic theories of the unconscious, behavior modification techniques, the development of psychophysical correlations in medicine and biochemistry, the Death of God movement in theology—such concepts have dominated the Western search for self, producing an ever more common belief that the sciences (natural and social) hold the key to our self-understanding. Certainly, however traumatic the psychological effects, the growth in the scientific knowledge of ourselves and our world has been staggering. It would be anachronistic for any view of the person to deny, for example, that anger can be described physiologically, that behavior can be modified through positive and negative conditioning, or that computers are theoretically capable of outstripping human thought in virtually all dimensions.

Yet a fundamental question remains. To what extent should scientific knowledge of the human world affect our definition of the person? A pervasive theme in phenomenology is that meaning depends on perspective. The ocean has a different meaning to the oceanographer studying plankton growth, the anthropologist studying island cultures, and the surfer studying a wave. Similarly, the meaning of humanity varies with one's standpoint and disposition. Acknowledging the importance of methodology in structuring un-derstanding, the West developed three domains within which hu-. mankind and the world are studied: the natural sciences, the social sciences, and the humanities (or, as they were more classically called, the human sciences). The rationale behind the trifurcation assumed that literary, artistic, historical, philosophical, and reli-gious studies collectively make a unique contribution to our under-standing. But in this age of scientism, we may lose sight of that unique contribution.

The Socratic quest to "know thyself" requires more than an in-crease in knowledge. It also involves a direct awareness of the seat of one's actions, the source of one's thought. This self-awareness is not itself conceptual, but it assumes a conceptual form when it is expressed in a historical and cultural context. This contextual ex-pression is the focus of humanistic studies. While the scientist discovers the universal by comparing individuals and abstracting common properties, the humanist finds the universal by delving into the particular. Consider, for example, Shakespeare's *Hamlet*. Regardless of our own ethnic and historical situation, we can be drawn into Hamlet's world, so much so that we identify with him. When I asked a Japanese friend why Shakespeare is so popular even among the Japanese (who know his work mostly through translation), he replied that Shakespeare is universal because he is so perfectly Elizabethan. In other words, the humanist (of whatever discipline) can create for us another way of seeing the world. How is this possible? The artistry of the humanist returns us to what we are before being conditioned by our historical and cultural situa-tion. In so doing, we encounter the immediate presence of things as they are and, having set aside our former assumptions, we empa-thize with another way of structuring that presence.

Even from these brief remarks, one can imagine how a Zen humanism might be outlined. It would involve knowledge of the person as a creative, spontaneous expression within specific cultural and historical manifestations. Before elaborating this notion, how-ever, we must first ask how such a Zen humanism can be intro-duced into the Western context. There is one obvious answer. This book itself is a presentation of Zen for a Western audience. Writers like D. T. Suzuki and Alan Watts have already influenced aspects of Western society from psychotherapy to poetry, from literature to religion. What is the problem then? As we have seen, any reflective account of a prereflective experience, even the one presented in this book, is structurally different from the experience itself. Up to the present, Westerners have been influenced more by the description of Zen than by Zen Buddhism itself. Imagine this hypothetical parallel.

Suppose an alien world sent to earth an observer who noted that earthlings did things much as they did, but with one notable exception. The earthlings engaged in a strange enterprise called "art." The alien brought back to his home planet no examples, but he did give a most enthusiastic account of it. The idea of art became a popular item of discussion in the alien world, especially among intellectuals, students, and coffee shop patrons. Books on the subject were instant bestsellers, and finally a few prints were brought from earth. Dissatisfied with having only photographic reprints of oil paintings and watercolors, the aliens finally arranged for a few painters to come to their planet. Although they were welcomed enthusiastically, the painters were soon disconsolate in their new home. The aliens seemed more interested in lectures on art than in learning to paint. Certainly, a few students did come around to the studios, but since artworks were virtually unknown in the alien culture, the students could only model themselves directly after their teachers' work. Ignorant of the range of forms art might take, the students could not distinguish greatness from mediocrity. The painters were also dismayed at the awesome task of introducing art to an artless culture. Art was important on earth in a fashion that could never be matched in this alien world, at least not until art permeated the society. In short, the artists only knew how to be artists in a world that already appreciated art and was pervasively influenced by it.

Though overstated for effect, this analogy does bring to light some of the technical difficulties involved in Zen Buddhism's transmission to the West. For Zen Buddhism to have any lasting effect on us, it must be more than an intellectual import.

## ZEN IN THE WEST

Can Zen Buddhism be directly transplanted into Western society today? Can it exert an influence in our society as powerful as the one it has exerted in Japan? If Zen Buddhism is to become a major influence in Western life, it will have to be transformed, not merely transplanted. Japanese culture is sufficiently different from ours that a Western disciple of Zen cannot be trained in exactly the same way as a Japanese. As we have seen, the Westerner generally has a different self-image from his or her Japanese counterpart. Specifically, Western individualism allows one to retain self-identity in radically different settings; in Japan, one's identity tends to be socially defined and it is expected to change from context to context. This does not mean, of course, that no Westerner can ever become an authentic Zen Buddhist. Individual differences may outweigh cultural influence. For a few Westerners, a traditional Zen Buddhist training may be highly effective, but we cannot expect *Japanese* Zen Buddhism to become a major religious force in the West. For similar reasons, perhaps, Christianity has never taken hold in Japan.

Still, the fundamental perspective of Zen Buddhism is acultural: it involves no necessary connection with a historical religious personage nor a faith in a fixed sacred reality articulated in a revelatory text. Zen Buddhism might, therefore, be so transformed as to be accessible to a greater number of Westerners. In Japan, despite the outreach of Zen to the laity (especially Sōtō Zen), Zen Buddhism is still primarily a monastic tradition. We have seen a good reason for this: monastic life establishes the uniquely Zen environment of nothingness out of which the Zen disciple will derive personal meaning. But, as we have just noted, context generally plays a more dominant role in determining personal meaning in Japan than in the West. Thus, in developing its more layperson-directed form, a Western Zen might not only be accessible to more people. It might also adapt to the individualism found in Western secular society.

Even with such transformations, Zen Buddhism may never become a prominent Western religious movement, but it could still be influential. Its very presence in our society can sensitize us to the value of contemplation—especially the Zen form of meditation. Although there might not be many who would characterize themselves as Zen Buddhists, a larger part of our population might someday be exposed to zazen and thereby recognize the prereflective as the ground of all experience. Zazen as a personal practice can also supplement other forms of religious activity. This development has already begun, in fact; many Christian monastic communities participate in zazen retreats, for example. To an ever greater extent, Western contemplatives see zazen as a means of revitalizing their own traditions.

In short, even though Zen Buddhism itself shows no signs of becoming a major Western religious tradition, its distinctive practice of zazen may yet add an important dimension to the spiritual life of non-Buddhists. If the Zen evaluation of prereflective experience were to become a prominent part of the Western tradition, how might the Western view of the person be affected? Before speculating on this question, let us first examine Zen's influence on a humanistic movement in modern Japan.

## MORITA THERAPY: ZEN HUMANISM IN MODERN JAPAN

As a young man, MORITA Shōma (1874–1938) was interested in Freudian psychoanalysis, but he eventually developed his own, uniquely Japanese, form of psychotherapy. The Zen Buddhist influence on Morita therapy is complex: although Morita himself denied any direct Zen influence and preferred to name Ludwig Binswanger, Wier Mitchell, and Paul Dubois as his predecessors,[1] he did have training in zazen, frequently quoted the great Zen Masters, and used Zen-influenced terminology.[2] In this way, Morita exemplifies what we may increasingly see in the West: a person trained in zazen who does not consider himself or herself a Zen Buddhist and yet develops a humanistic theory with a distinctively Zen perspective.

To appreciate Morita's theory as a humanism, let us see how early Western theories were more scientific in orientation. For brevity, we will consider only the two figures having the most sustained influence: Freud and Jung.[3] In the Freudian model, neurosis arises from repressing the memory of a psychically traumatic event. Freud developed various techniques (dream interpretation and free association, for example) by which the analyst could bypass the ego's defense mechanisms and bring the repressed data to consciousness. The goal of Freudian therapy is, therefore, abreaction: the psychic reenactment of that traumatic event in order to release the tension accrued from it and from the repression of its memory. This allows the patient to recall the previous traumatic event and to *express the painful affect in words.*[4] In a Freudian analysis, the analysand seeks self-understanding: the explanation of one's present neurotic behavior by articulation of a repressed memory. The cure follows upon this reflective understanding.

In short, Freud's psychoanalytic therapy is retrospective and reflective in character. It is retrospective in its goal of making the past available to present consciousness. It is reflective in two respects. From the analyst's standpoint, theoretical structures (ego/id/superego; conscious/unconscious/preconscious; the symbolism of dreams interpreted as the wish-fulfillment of the libido) are used to explain the patient's behavior and motivations. From the patient's standpoint, the cure comes about through an articulated, conceptual understanding of forgotten events causing the present neurosis. In other words, Freudian therapy arises out of etiology and, to this extent, is scientific in orientation.

Jung's model is also scientific in this regard, although it differs in two major aspects. First, it is prospective rather than retrospective. Second, its scientific model is more organic than mechanistic. Let us briefly examine how this is so. Jung believed the psyche, like any other organism, tends to cure itself if unhindered by external forces. That is, when a neurotic imbalance develops, the psyche has a natural tendency to right itself.[5] This propensity reveals itself through archetypal symbols appearing in dreams, hallucinations, and the imagination. A competent Jungian analyst interprets these symbols in order to reveal the psyche's attempt to establish an equilibrium among thinking, feeling, intuition, and sensation. Hence, Jungian analysis is prospective in seeking that toward which the psyche is developing. Its goal is to eliminate all obstructions to that process.

Despite this divergence from Freud, Jungian therapy is nevertheless primarily reflective. A cure is achieved only through a conceptual analysis of the patient's archetypal experiences. The interpretation is formulated in terms of a previously established theory. While Jung's approach may be more like the organic treatment of a physician and Freud's more like the repair work of an engineer, both are reflective and quasi-scientific in spirit in emphasizing etiology, reflective interpretation, and predetermined sets of heuristic categories. Morita's Zen-influenced form of psychotherapy has a different character, however.

Morita therapy is directed primarily toward a group of hypochondriacal conditions generally characterized as "nervosity" or "nervousness" (shinkeishitsu)—the specific symptoms range from headaches or insomnia to fears of interpersonal contact and even a phobia for dirt. The disorder generally afflicts introverted, intelligent, goal-directed perfectionists who are overly self-conscious and critical of their own feelings and thoughts. Morita holds that the self-conscious focus on one's own psychological states is perfectly normal. Trouble begins only when one is "caught" (toraware) in this mode and the flow of consciousness is blocked. Some minor malady captures one's attention, becomes a fixation and, consequently, the basis for hypochondria. The more one concentrates on one's symptoms, the worse they become.

A hallmark of Morita therapy is its lack of attempting any cure. The goal is to have the patient accept the given without concern for what should be. If one cannot sleep, one does not exacerbate the situation by thinking one should be able to do so. Taking the insomnia as a given, one simply goes on with one's affairs. Similarly, one is advised to accept emotions as they arise; one is responsible for actions, not feelings. Morita therapists use the example of jumping off a high diving board.[6] How one feels about jumping is irrelevant. If one is fearful, one accepts that fear and jumps anyway. The fear is "just what is" (arugamama), and one does not analyze it for either causes in the past or anticipations of what the future will bring. One just acts. The therapy itself begins with a week of complete bed rest: no activities whatsoever are allowed. One is told simply to think what one thinks and to feel what one feels. Eventually, the patient develops a desire to perform some activity and is gradually given increasingly complex duties (starting with raking the leaves in the garden, for example). Finally, one reaches the point when one can see what has to be done on one's own initiative.

Although this is only a brief sketch, it is enough to show how Morita therapy is related to Zen humanism. This relation has four major aspects. First, the therapy is not scientific in that its goals—self-awareness and action—are achieved without passing through the intermediate stage of theoretical self-understanding. Morita therapists are basically uninterested in either etiology or cure.[7] Thus, patients are given no theory through which to understand their neurosis. One is trained to see what is and what needs to be done; then one simply acts accordingly. Second, Morita therapy is present-directed rather than retrospective or prospective. For the healthy person, retrospection and prospection are normal ways of reflecting on one's own activity, but for someone suffering from *shinkeishitsu*, they are ways of becoming caught *(toraware)* in intellection and of neurotically postponing action. Third, Morita ultimately defines the person in terms of action. One learns to see oneself as what one does. In fact, a Morita patient keeps a daily diary—not of feelings, thoughts, or desires, but of the actions one actually performs each day.

Finally, self-consciousness, even as a reflective mode, is accepted as a natural part of human life. What causes suffering, however, is being trapped in self-reflection. The neurosis of *shinkeishitsu* is much like the suffering Zen finds in everyday, unenlightened consciousness—namely, one thinks about thinking and tries futilely to break this cycle by thinking more. Analysis, whether of the self or of the world, can never end; a new distinction is always possible. One becomes decreasingly responsive in one's actions as one understands oneself to be an agent independent of the experiential process. The way out of the vicious cycle is to forget the self and return to what is—*arugamama* or, in Dōgen's terms, *genjōkōan*. Bearing in mind this contemporary Japanese example of a non-

Buddhist application of Zen humanism,* we can now return to our
own situation. How might a Zen humanism be applied to present
Western concerns?

## ZEN HUMANISM FOR THE WEST

As we noted at the beginning of this chapter, the traditional
Western view of the person has suffered from the rise of scientism.
In many respects, traditional humanism operated within medieval,
scholastic categories. We thought of the person as having a uniquely human essence transcending all physical, contingent characteristics. This essence was considered not only the source of our
humanity but also the seat of free will. In short, the traditional
Western notion affirmed a *soul*, or at least a spirit. It is significant,
however, that the medieval triad of body, mind, and soul has gradually given way to the modern dyad of body and mind. Originally,
the term *mind*, as in the German word *Geist*, contained the notion
of both mind and spirit, but the thrust of scientism has been to
eliminate the spiritual component entirely. The Darwinian argues,
for example, that our animal ancestors had no spirit. Hence how
could a component so distinctive evolve from the lower species?
Cybernetics regards the computer as an electronic mind, the
assumption often being that *spirit*, whatever the anachronists mean
by that word, is just an intricate function qualitatively no different
from ordinary cognitive acts. Behaviorists like B. F. Skinner reduce
spirit to complex conditioned responses that, once understood, will
obviate the need for humanistic ideals like dignity and freedom.
Even more perniciously, these scientific standpoints often reduce
not only spirit to mind, but even mind to body. In this regard, the
social sciences are losing ground to the natural sciences. To main-

---

*This is not to say that Morita therapy perfectly matches the Zen Buddhist ideal. In
the first place, Morita therapy lacks the Zen emphasis on creativity. Moreover, it
draws a strong distinction between actions and feelings, claiming success when the
patient is able to function again even if the psychological trauma continues. In this
sense, Zen Buddhism is different in that it does try to cure the psychological pain as
well. In fact, all forms of Buddhism share the ideal of alleviating human suffering.

tain their scientific respectability, they have become increasingly quantitative.

Even the humanities, in self-defense perhaps, have sought ever greater objectivity and scientific distance. In philosophy, for example, there is an emphasis on the logical study of language, and the positivists have suggested that all empirically unverifiable claims should be expurgated from philosophical discourse. In the literary realm, the New Criticism centers on the completed literary document; the author's creative intent and personal circumstances are irrelevant. In the study of religion, the emphasis has shifted from the articulation of religious sentiments to the linguistic analysis of texts, the objective reporting of religious behavior, and the accumulation of historical facts. Even on the popular level, biblical literalism reads scripture like a science textbook rather than as a creative expression of religious aspiration in the light of revelation.

Because many of the basic ideas about the self were thus reevaluated in light of scientific discoveries, an either/or alternative emerged: either we affirm the person as something totally outside scientific understanding (a view taken by some personalists and existentialists, for example) or we let our view of the person be defined totally in terms of scientific understanding (as, for instance, in behaviorism). But does this have to be the case? Is there not a way to reformulate our humanism so that it at once affirms traditional values and also recognizes the truth of scientific discoveries? The Zen humanism we have been investigating suggests such a possibility. While the humanities have increasingly focused on the final product of human activity, Zen is both refreshing and provoking in its emphasis on the source, not the end result, of the human act.

For Zen, body, mind, and spirit are not three substantially different entities; rather, they are three profiles of the person that are determined by perspective. In our culture, the natural sciences focus mainly on the body, the social sciences on the mind, the humanities on the spirit. The natural scientist stands in the physical world and sees the human being as a continuous part of it. Such a perspective understands human activity to be governed by natural laws. The social scientist, on the other hand, sees the human being

as *homo faber*—one who has realized in practice the concepts of a
given time and place. From this standpoint, the observer tries to
isolate the conscious and unconscious frameworks structuring the
human world. The humanities center on the creative enterprise
itself: the way in which human needs, desires, and ideas take form
in different historical and cultural contexts. Another way of characterizing these differences is to say the natural sciences examine the
human being as a product (of physical and organic forces); the
social sciences study a human product (the social world); and the
humanities study human producing (artistic, moral, religious, and
philosophical ideals).

Zen *humanism* does not, however, mean the Zen view of the person affirms the standpoint of the humanities over that of the natural and social sciences. Any form of knowledge is reflective and,
therefore, of secondary concern. In emphasizing the prereflective
ground of all experience, Zen is prescientific and prehumanistic.
Thus, zazen might be of interest to a natural scientist for its
physiological implications or to a social scientist for its social
relevance in Japan. This book is representative of the humanities
in its investigation of the philosophical implications of zazen. Still,
Zen Buddhism might object to scientism even though it has no
quarrel with science per se. Scientism is reductionistic: it claims
that the scientific perspective is the only valid one. In Morita's
terms, the scientistic view is *caught* in its own conceptualization.
Science is capable of discovering great truths about humanity and
its world, but any truth achieved through reflection is dependent on
context.

As Dōgen pointed out, the ocean indeed is a translucent palace
to a fish and a necklace of glittering jewels to a deva in heaven.
Given their standpoints, each account is true. Difficulties only
arise, for example, when the fish believes that the translucence of
the ocean proves the deva wrong in seeing it as glittering. We desire a theory of the world and of the person which is true from all
perspectives, but no theory can ever meet this criterion. We cannot
transcend the fact that we are spatially, temporally, culturally, and
linguistically determinate. Every reflective truth is an expression
not only of what is but also of *how* it is from a specific viewpoint.

This is why Zen Buddhism advocates the context of *mu*. To be freely responsive, to act as the situation demands, one must have no
vested interest in a conceptual scheme. Having one's meaning as a
person tied to no context, one can express each situation or occasion *(jisetsu)* as it is.

In the final analysis, the Zen person has no *intrinsic* meaning:
there is no person at all. As each context arises, however, the Zen
person is the response to what is, as it is. The act is an expression
in a context; it is the meaning of the Zen person for that time,
place, and situation. Grounded in the prereflective base of experience, the Zen Buddhist changes his or her meaning as the contexts
change. Hence, the tradition speaks of human freedom as being like
clouds or water—continually altering form to fit surrounding
circumstances.

For such a Zen humanism to take hold in the West, we would
have to relinquish certain beliefs. Above all, we must recognize
that no theory can ever explain everything. Every discursive account depends on the context. This notion is easy to accept in
abstraction, but difficult to realize in practice. The psychological
obstruction is not simply a desire for omniscience, a wish to be
God. As the Buddhists point out, the cause of our dogmatism, in-
flexibility, and suffering is our craving for permanence, especially
personal permanence. We want truth to be cumulative so that what
is learned as true today will also be true tomorrow, even though
the context changes. We fancy ourselves at the center of a fixed and
absolute worldview. Our commitment to this ideal of the static self
is the source of our anxiety. Change is painful in proportion to our
resistance to it. If we cease desiring the permanent, all-inclusive
Truth, will we not be flexible enough to express the truth in each
situation? Because our resistance to Zen humanism is psychological
and practical, not theoretical, to understand Zen Buddhism intellec-
tually is not enough. For Zen to affect the West in any significant
and lasting fashion, Zen practice, not Zen theory, must be inter-
nalized into our culture. Zazen is central because in it action and
being are one: one is what one does. The Zen person is inseparable
from Zen action.

In conclusion, if Westerners commit themselves to the practice of zazen (or any other contemplative practice, Eastern or Western, emphasizing prereflective experience), there will be a gradual reorientation in our notion of the person. We will be less comfortable with theories that take the person to be a closed system, whether that system be posed in terms taken from the humanities or the sciences. We will, moreover, appreciate the mystery at the base of experience. This mystery is not an obscure realm like the unconscious: something unfathomable and never experienced directly. Rather, it is a mystery in a more technically religious sense. That is, the prereflective ground of experience is immediately encountered in even the most mundane of experiences, but it cannot be articulated conceptually without thereby limiting its richness. Articulation is by no means *wrong*; in fact, it is an accomplishment of our species as it effects the creative adjustment of the world to our needs, and our needs to the world. But any expression, however true, is limited.

The genuine person—the person who intrinsically has no standpoint—takes a specific perspective in order to achieve an expression of what is. This free act of creation underlies the formulations of both the sciences and the humanities. The goal of Zen humanism is to appreciate the wondrous power of this act while being aware of the limitations of the context which makes the expression possible. To be Rinzai's person of no status, to be Enō's original face, to be Dōgen's primordial person is to be essentially no person, while simultaneously being the personal act appropriate to the occasion.

| | |
|---|---|
| *Kono michi ya* | Ah, this path. |
| *Yukuhito nashi ni* | With no person travelling it, |
| *Aki no kure.*[8] | An autumn twilight. |
| | —Bashō |

# Notes

CHAPTER 1 / THE CULTURAL SETTING: CONTEXT AND
PERSONAL MEANING

   1. In fact, there is a classic example of such a Japanese analysis of man,
WATSUJI Tetsurō's *Rinrigaku* [Ethics], most readily available in vols. 10
and 11 of his *Zenshū* [Complete works]. Originally begun in the early
1930s, this work was written, in part, as a response to Heidegger's *Being
and Time*. In Watsuji's eyes, Heidegger erred in emphasizing the individuality of *Dasein* over the collectivity of *Mitsein*, the most tragic outcome being Heidegger's inability to treat the ethical dimension of humanity. In effect, Watsuji's project is to reverse Heidegger's approach by making the
*Mitsein* the starting point for his existential, phenomenological analysis.
Since Heidegger hermeneutically analyzes various German words for man
such as *Mensch* and *man*, Watsuji centers on the Japanese word for human
being, *ningen*, showing that it presupposes man *(hito, NIN)* in a context of
betweenness *(GEN)*. The first short chapter of Watsuji's work has been
translated by David Dilworth: "The Significance of Ethics of the Study of
Man," *Monumenta Nipponica* 26(3-4)(1971):395-413.
   2. NAKAMURA Hajime, *Ways of Thinking of Eastern Peoples*, p. 409.
   3. SHIBAYAMA Zenkei, *Zen Comments on the Mumonkan*, p. 19.
   4. Insofar as Jōshū seems to have no alternative—either an affirmative or
negative response is subject to criticism—this is a double-bind situation.
Bateson describes this phenomenon in familial behavior, where it precipi-
tates schizophrenia in children. Of course, unlike the child, Jōshū is able to
transcend the double bind. This point will be developed in our later discussion of koan practice. For an explanation of the double-bind theory, see
Gregory Bateson, "Toward a Theory of Schizophrenia," in *Steps to an
Ecology of Mind*. On p. 208, Bateson makes a brief reference to Zen
koans.
   5. The "yes-and-no" here translates the Chinese *yu-wu*, which could also

be rendered "being-and-not-being," "there-is-and-there-is-not [Buddha-nature]," or "[the puppy] has-and-has-not [Buddha-nature]."
  6. Shibayama, *Mumonkan*, p. 20.
  7. Ibid., pp. 19–20.
  8. Philip Kapleau, ed. and trans., *The Three Pillars of Zen*, pp. 79–80.
  9. Shibayama, *Mumonkan*, pp. 21–22.
  10. Ibid., p. 22.
  11. SASAKI Joshu Roshi, *Buddha Is the Center of Gravity*, p. 22. It should be noted that Zen Masters do not traditionally refer to "God," but Sasaki is adapting his message to an American audience.
  12. Ibid., p. 27.
  13. Shibayama, *Mumonkan*, p. 22.

## CHAPTER 2 / NĀGĀRJUNA: THE LOGIC OF EMPTINESS

  1. A clear, concise discussion of abhidharmic scholasticism is presented by David J. Kalupahana, *Buddhist Philosophy*, chap. 9.
  2. T. R. V. Murti, *Central Philosophy of Buddhism*, p. 13.
  3. This rendering is adapted from an unpublished translation by David J. Kalupahana. A translation of the entire *MK* is found in Frederick J. Streng, *Emptiness*, pp. 183–200. A more technical translation with the original text is Kenneth K. Inada, *Nāgārjuna*.
  4. For a valuable clarification of Nāgārjuna's understanding of concepts, see chap. 11 of Kalupahana, *Buddhist Philosophy*.
  5. Streng, *Emptiness*, p. 52.
  6. Ibid., p. 39.
  7. Original Japanese taken from Daniel C. Buchanan, trans., *One Hundred Famous Haiku*, p. 89. (My translation.)

## CHAPTER 3 / CHINESE TAOISM: THE PRE-ONTOLOGY OF NONBEING

  1. Lao Tzŭ's dates are still a matter of disagreement. Holmes Welch *[Taoism]* and FUNG Yu-lan [*History of Chinese Philosophy*, vol. 1] assign him to the early or middle fourth century B.C. Chuang Tzŭ, on the other hand, probably lived in the late fourth and early third centuries B.C.
  2. For a brief treatment of the historical development of the term *tao*, see CHANG Chung-yuan, *Creativity and Taoism*, pp. 24–28.
  3. Translations of *Tao Tê Ching* are taken from CHANG Chung-yuan, *Tao: A New Way of Thinking*. This translation utilizes the commentarial tradition but is distinctively philosophical in both translation and notes. Other translations consulted include: Wing-tsit CHAN, *The Way of Lao Tzu*; Lao Tsu, *Tao Te Ching*, trans. FENG Gia-Fu and Jane English; Arthur Waley, *The Way and Its Power*.
  4. Quoted in Chang, *Creativity and Taoism*, p. 51.

5. Chuang Tzu, *The Complete Works of Chuang Tzu*, trans. Burton Watson, p. 40.

6. Ibid., p. 131.

7. Max Kaltenmark, *Lao Tzu and Taoism*, p. 40. For consistency of reference, quoted interpolations appear in parentheses throughout this book whereas my own are enclosed in brackets.

8. Wing-tsit CHAN, *The Way*, p. 7.

9. *Chuang Tzu*, p. 244.

10. For a discussion of Taoist meditation techniques, see Chang, *Creativity and Taoism*, pp. 47-50 and 123-168.

11. Original Japanese taken from Bashō, *Back Roads to Far Towns*, p. 98. (My translation.)

## CHAPTER 4 / NO-MIND: THE ZEN RESPONSE TO NOTHINGNESS

1. For example, in times when Buddhism was under attack in China, the distinction between the two terms was sometimes emphasized, the *wu* being considered an indigenous, traditional concept contrasted with the "foreign" (Indian) influenced idea of *k'ung*.

2. For a classic anthropological study of responsibility in very traditional Japanese social structures, see Ruth Benedict, *The Chrysanthemum and the Sword*, especially chaps. 5-10.

3. Shibayama, *Mumonkan*, case 7, p. 67.

4. Ibid., pp. 68-69.

5. Ibid., p. 26.

6. Ibid., p. 69.

7. Philip B. Yampolsky, trans., *The Platform Sutra of the Sixth Patriarch*, pp. 137-138.

8. Ibid., p. 138.

9. Garma C. C. CHANG, *The Practice of Zen*, p. 86.

10. UCHIYAMA Kosho Roshi, *Approach to Zen*, pp. 30-31.

11. A variation of this story is found in Paul Reps, comp., *Zen Flesh, Zen Bones*, p. 14.

12. Daisetz Teitaro SUZUKI, *The Zen Doctrine of No-Mind*, p. 75.

13. Sasaki, *Buddha*, p. 29.

14. All page references refer to Martin Heidegger, *Discourse on Thinking*, trans. John M. Anderson and E. Hans Freund (New York: Harper & Row, 1966).

15. SUZUKI Daisetsu, *Rinzai no kihonshisō* [The fundamental ideas of Rinzai], pp. 15-18.

16. Translation (with slight alterations) taken from Erich Fromm, D. T. Suzuki, and Richard DeMartino, *Zen Buddhism and Psychoanalysis*, p. 32. Alterations suggested by Suzuki's Japanese version in *Rinzai*, p. 15.

17. Suzuki, *Rinzai*, p. 16. (In Japanese.)

18. Yampolsky, *Platform Sutra*, p. 110.

19. Original Japanese taken from Buchanan, *Hundred Famous Haiku*, p. 88. (My translation.)

## CHAPTER 5 / ZEN AND REALITY

1. The Zen view implies that any discussion of the historical development of human consciousness is restricted to the way various *reflective* structures have been revised throughout history to suit the philosophical needs of a given culture in a specific period. Because of their emphasis on nonreflective aspects of consciousness, Zen Buddhists are seldom interested in such discussions: the enlightenment of a modern Zen Master in Japan is considered essentially the same as the enlightenment of the Buddha in India 2500 years ago. Because of their different physical circumstances, the Buddha and the Zen Master may use different expressions in teaching, but the source of their expressions is considered to be the same. The relationship between historical conditions and nonhistorical insight is examined in Chapter 9.

2. John Dewey, *The Quest for Certainty*, pp. 16–17.

3. To overcome the problems inherent in these terminological tensions, one Western strategy has been dialectics, a way of accepting the intrinsic tendency of conceptual systems to lead "logically" to their contradictories. This approach usually assumes that the statement of the function of the dialectic is a statement about the *rest* of conceptualization. That is, the dialectic itself cannot be called into question dialectically—to do so would jeopardize the very rationale for asserting the dialectic in the first place. This dialectical view is susceptible to a Nāgārjunan attack: the term *dialectics* depends on other terms for its definition, including ideas diametrically opposed to dialectics. If dialectics involves the modification of all ideas, for example, then the dialectician is challenged to define that notion without it itself being modified. If the challenge cannot be met, the dialectician's very claim to intelligibility is undercut.

4. NISHIDA Kitarō, *A Study of Good*, pp. 1–2. The original text is available in NISHIDA Kitarō, *Zen no kenkyū*, included in *Nihon no meicho* [Famous works of Japan], vol. 47.

5. Ibid., pp. 1–4.

6. Ibid., p. 7.

7. Ibid., p. 12.

8. Jean-Paul Sartre, *The Transcendence of the Ego*, p. 45.

9. Nishida, *Study of Good*, p. 16.

10. In this regard, it is interesting that both Nishida and Sartre recognize our inability to be reflectively conscious of the presently existing self. For Nishida, the consequence of this observation is that all experience is immediate and a reflective analysis can never come to grips with that immediacy. Hence all experience is *pure*. Taking a more Cartesian stance,

Sartre holds that knowledge can only arise out of the reflective understanding of the self. Since reflection cannot know the present self, I can never know who I am. Therefore I am doomed, to a certain extent, to living in *bad faith*. Our interest here is that the two philosophers share a common analysis and conclusion. But Nishida, seeing an affirmation of Zen, rejoices in the purity of experience whereas Sartre, seeing a rejection of the Cartesian analysis of truth, feels the despair of bad faith.

11. William James, "A World of Pure Experience," p. 25.

*CHAPTER 6 / DŌGEN'S PHENOMENOLOGY OF ZAZEN*

1. Hee-jin KIM, *Dōgen Kigen—Mystical Realist*, p. 21. Kim gives a good summary of Dōgen's biography in chap. 2.

2. Ibid., p. 25.

3. In this regard, the Western reader may be reminded of Martin Heidegger. As Heidegger's etymological discussions of Greek and German philosophical terms (whether scientifically accurate or not) help us to see philosophical language in a new and creative way, Dōgen too returns to the basic meanings of Chinese characters and thereby makes seemingly innocuous, traditional, passages come alive with profoundly Zen meaning.

4. See ABE Masao, "Dōgen on Buddha Nature," pp. 30–31.

5. Dōgen's treatment of the phrase *shoakumakusa* is explained in Chapter 7.

6. Norman Waddell and ABE Masao, trans., "Dōgen's Fukanzazengi and Shōbōgenzō Zazengi," pp. 122–123. For consistency with our discussion, I have made three minor changes: "without-thinking" for "non-thinking," "cultivation-authentication" for "practice-realization," and "presence of things as they are" for "manifestation of ultimate reality."

7. None of these terms should be confused with "no-thought" or "no-mind" as discussed in Chapter 4. Although "without-thinking" is close in spirit to these terms, it is explicitly related to "thinking" and "not-thinking."

8. DŌGEN Kigen, *Dōgen zenji zenshū* [Complete works of Zen Master Dōgen], vol. 1, p. 90. (In Japanese.)

9. TAKAHASHI Masanobu, *Shōbōgenzō*, p. 128. (In Japanese.)

10. TERADA Tōru and MIZUNO Yaoko, *Dōgen*, vol. 1, p. 128. (In Japanese.)

11. AKIYAMA Hanji, *Dōgen no kenkyū* [A study of Dōgen], p. 256. (In Japanese.)

12. Ibid., p. 256.

13. Ibid., p. 256.

14. Ibid., p. 256.

15. Ibid., p. 257.

16. Akiyama also suggests a noetic-noematic analysis (in *Dōgen*, pp. 255 ff.), but it has a somewhat different emphasis than the one discussed

here. A major point of similarity is that Akiyama characterizes the act aspect as "nothingness" *(mu)* and the content aspect as "being" *(u)*.

17. In French existentialism, too, especially in Merleau-Ponty and Marcel, there is an attempt to recapture the true nature of prereflective experience.

18. We recall Akiyama's saying the relationships among thinking, not-thinking, and without-thinking are "dialectical," that without-thinking "sublates" thinking and not-thinking. Insofar as without-thinking does not arise from the interplay between thinking and not-thinking but, in fact, is the basis out of which the two arise, this cannot be considered a dialectical relationship in the Hegelian sense. Perhaps Akiyama had Nishida's dialectic in mind. If so, the sublation of thinking and not-thinking is strictly logical and not temporal; that is, thinking and not-thinking have meaning only within the larger domain of without-thinking. In Nishida's terminology, without-thinking gives thinking and not-thinking a logical "place" *(basho)*.

We also note in passing that our account of without-thinking parallels the Taoist characterization of Nonbeing described in Chapter 3. For Taoism, distinctionless Nonbeing is the source of the division into affirmative Being and its counterpart, Nonbeing; for Dōgen, nonobjectifying without-thinking is the source of objectifying thinking and its negation, not-thinking.

19. Dōgen, *Zenshū*, vol. 1, p. 9. (In Japanese.) Compare Norman Waddell and ABE Masao, trans., "Shōbōgenzō Genjōkōan," p. 137.

20. Dōgen, *Zenshū*, p. 737. (In Japanese.) Compare Norman Waddell and ABE Masao, trans., "Dōgen's Bendōwa," pp. 147–148.

21. Waddell and Abe, "Bendōwa," pp. 136–137. Compare Dōgen, *Zenshū*, vol. 1, p. 732. Again, for consistency with our text, "cultivation" was substituted for "practice" and "authentication" for "realization."

22. For a discussion of Nāgārjuna's argument for the interdependence of temporal distinctions, see Chapter 2.

23. Dōgen, *Zenshū*, vol. 1, p. 191. (In Japanese.)

24. Waddell and Abe, "Genjōkōan," p. 135.

25. Abe, "Buddha Nature," p. 66.

26. Virtually the same issue was raised in our discussion of Nāgārjuna in Chapter 2, where we questioned whether his position would lead to either an essentialist or a nonessentialist view of the person. The perspectives taken by Nāgārjuna and Dōgen are fundamentally different, however, in that Nāgārjuna is *logical* or epistemological (incorporating an analysis of the logical interdependence of opposing philosophical terms), but Dōgen is *phenomenological* (utilizing an interpretation of the structures of consciousness, especially as revealed in zazen).

27. See the discussion of this phrase in the section "Dōgen's Philosophical Project."

28. See Abe, "Buddha Nature," p. 52.

29. Heinrich Dumoulin renders it "öffentliche Bekanntsmachung" or "öffentliche Aushang." See Dumoulin, "Das Buch Genjōkōan aus dem Shōbōgenzō des Zen Meisters Dōgen," p. 223.

30. Waddell and Abe, "Genjōkōan," p. 130.

31. Waddell and Abe, "Genjōkōan," p. 130; Dumoulin, "Genjōkōan," p. 223.

32. MASUNAGA Reihō, Eihei Shōbōgenzō, English section, p. 1; DESHIMARU Taisen, Shōbōgenzō, pp. 16-17; Kim, Dōgen, pp. 100-101.

33. Dumoulin, "Genjōkōan," p. 223. (In German.)

34. Dōgen, Zenshū, vol. 1, p. 191.

35. This example comes from the fascicle "Genjōkōan." See Dōgen, Zenshū, vol. 1, p. 9, and Waddell and Abe, "Genjōkōan," p. 137. The latter has a helpful footnote.

36. There is also a 95-fascicle version of Shōbōgenzō compiled by the Sōtō order after Dōgen's death.

CHAPTER 7 / DŌGEN: PERSON AS PRESENCE

1. DŌGEN Kigen, Dōgen zenji zenshū [Complete works of Zen Master Dōgen], vol. 1, pp. 7-8. (In Japanese.)

2. Ibid., p. 7. (In Japanese.)

3. This quotation is a common one located in such classic didactic texts as the Dhammapada (183). The passage also has special significance in the Japanese tradition in that it is said to be the death verse of Prince Shōtoku (A.D. 574-622), the great royal patron of Buddhism and the first major commentator on Buddhism in Japan. See Daigan Matsunaga and Alicia Matsunaga, Foundation of Japanese Buddhism, vol. 1, p. 12.

4. Dōgen, Zenshū, p. 278. (In Japanese.)

5. Ibid., p. 281. (In Japanese.)

6. Some intuitional theories of ethics approach the prereflective but fail to reach it. In other words, while intuition is a seemingly prereflective experience, insofar as it yields an intuition of the good (or any other objectified concept), Zen would not consider it truly without-thinking.

7. Paul Ricoeur, Husserl: An Analysis of His Phenomenology, p. 9.

8. Dōgen, Zenshū, vol. 2, p. 416. (In Japanese.)

CHAPTER 8 / HAKUIN: THE PSYCHODYNAMICS OF ZEN TRAINING

1. Philip B. Yampolsky, trans., The Zen Master Hakuin, p. 116.

2. Ibid., p. 117.

3. Ibid., p. 118.

4. Heinrich Dumoulin, A History of Zen Buddhism, p. 258.

5. Ibid., p. 258.

6. Yampolsky, Hakuin, pp. 135-136.

7. Ibid., pp. 118–119.
8. Dumoulin, *History*, p. 251.
9. Yampolsky, *Hakuin*, p. 119.
10. Dumoulin, *History*, p. 252.
11. Yampolsky, *Hakuin*, p. 120.
12. Ibid., p. 120.
13. The term *mokushō zen* has a long tradition in Zen. Hakuin uses it pejoratively to refer to Zen Buddhists who compulsively sit in meditation to purify the mind and escape from the activities of ordinary life. In China (where it is pronounced *mo-chao-ch'an*) this term was a central issue of debate between its advocate, Tien-t'ung, and its critic, Ta-hui. See Dumoulin, *History*, pp. 132 ff.
14. Yampolsky, *Hakuin*, p. 32.
15. Ibid., p. 58.
16. Ibid., p. 1.
17. SHIBAYAMA Zenkei, *A Flower Does Not Talk*, pp. 46–47.
18. See Chapter 1, note 4.
19. Shibayama, *Zen Comments on the Mumonkan*, p. 299.
20. Ibid., p. 301.
21. Shibayama, *Flower*, p. 33.
22. Yampolsky, *Hakuin*, p. 38.
23. See Shibayama, *Flower*, pp. 110–112.
24. See Henry Rosemont, Jr., "The Meaning Is the Use: *Kōan* and *Mondō* as Linguistic Tools of the Zen Masters," *Philosophy East and West*, 20(April 1970):109 ff. Rosemont argues that koans are often used with perlocutionary, rather than illocutionary, force.
25. Original Japanese as well as the background of this haiku are taken from R. H. Blyth, *Haiku*, vol. 4, p. 95. (My translation.)

## CHAPTER 9 / ZEN ACTION/ZEN PERSON

1. *Chuang Tzu*, chap. 25, p. 293.
2. For Zen Master Sasaki's brief discussion of the interpenetration of the "historical" and the "absolute" standpoints, see Sasaki, *Buddha*, pp. 29–31.
3. Psychological research indicates there is a physiological parallel to this "first-time" experience. One set of studies on zazen using electro-encephalograph readings (EEG) showed that the habituation pattern was radically altered in zazen. The test involved a periodic click repeated every fifteen seconds while two groups of people were seated quietly, one as a test sample, the other as representative of accomplished zazen practitioners. The EEG indicated that in the test group, after three or four clicks, the sound was gradually screened out by the brain until the clicks apparently had no effect on their consciousnesses. (The same habituation occurs when we cease to notice the ticking of a grandfather's clock after

a few moments.) For the Zen Master, however, the situation was markedly different. Even after five minutes, the EEG showed the same response as registered for the first click. Physiologically, each click was a first click. See Claudio Naranjo and Robert E. Ornstein, *On the Psychology of Meditation*, p. 196.

4. Martin Heidegger, *Poetry, Language, Thought*, p. 208.

5. Ibid., p. 6.

6. The Taoist term *wu-wei* was discussed in Chapter 3. Dōgen's use of the term *makusa* was treated in Chapter 7.

7. See Heidegger, *Poetry*, p. 210.

8. Nishida, *Zen no kenkyū*, p. 106. See also the English translation, *Study of Good*, p. 19.

9. Original Japanese taken from Buchanan, *Hundred Famous Haiku*, p. 16. (My translation.)

## CHAPTER 10 / PHILOSOPHICAL POSTSCRIPT: TOWARD A ZEN HUMANISM

1. David K. Reynolds, *Morita Psychotherapy*, p. 49.

2. For the argument that Morita is strongly influenced by Zen, see, for example, KORA Takehisa and SATO Koji, "Morita Therapy—A Psychotherapy in the Way of Zen," and SATO Koji, "Psychotherapeutic Implications of Zen," both in *Psychologia* 1(1958). L. Takeo Doi, "Morita Therapy and Psychoanalysis," *Psychologia* 5(1962):120-121, speculates on the political reasons for Morita's underplaying the influence of Zen.

3. For a more detailed comparison between Zen and these two Western figures, see my "Zen Buddhism, Freud, and Jung," *The Eastern Buddhist*, NS 10,1(May 1977):68-91.

4. For Freud's emphasis on verbalizing the repressed affect, see *Studies in Hysteria* (1895) in *The Standard Edition of the Complete Psychological Works of Sigmund Freud*, vol. 2, p. 255.

5. See Carl G. Jung, "The Transcendent Function" (1958), *The Collected Works of Carl G. Jung*, vol. 8, pp. 67-91.

6. See KORA Takehisa, "Morita Therapy," *Memorial Lectures for Professor Kora*, p. 10, and Reynolds, *Morita Psychotherapy*, pp. 167-168.

7. There are exceptions, however. L. Takeo Doi, for example, relates the arising of *shinkeishitsu* to a frustrated attempt to achieve *amaeru*, dependence on another's love. See KAKETA Katsumi, "Psychoanalysis in Japan," *Psychologia* 1(1958):250-251. For a concise discussion of *amaeru*, see L. Takeo Doi, "Amae: A Key Concept for Understanding Japanese Personality Structure," in *Japanese Culture and Behavior*, pp. 145-154. Reynolds also suggests his own etiology based on the concept of *enryo* in chap. 3 of *Morita Psychotherapy*.

8. Original Japanese taken from Harold G. Henderson, *An Introduction to Haiku*, p. 48. (My translation.)

# Works Cited

Abe, Masao. "Dōgen on Buddha Nature." *The Eastern Buddhist*, NS 4, 1(1971):28–71.

Akiyama Hanji. *Dōgen no kenkyū* [A study of Dōgen]. Tokyo: Iwanami Shoten, 1935.

Bashō. *Back Roads to Far Towns: Basho's Oku-No-Hosomichi*. Translated by Cid Corman and Susumu Kamaike. New York: Grossman Publishers, 1968.

Bateson, Gregory. "Toward a Theory of Schizophrenia." In *Steps to an Ecology of Mind*. New York: Ballantine Books, 1972.

Benedict, Ruth. *The Chrysanthemum and the Sword: Patterns of Japanese Culture*. Rutland, Vermont: Charles E. Tuttle, 1946.

Blyth, R. H. *Haiku*. 4 vols. Tokyo: Hokuseido, 1952.

Buchanan, Daniel C., trans. *One Hundred Famous Haiku*. San Francisco: Japan Publications, 1973.

Chan, Wing-tsit. *The Way of Lao Tzu*. New York: Bobbs-Merrill, 1963.

Chang, Chung-yuan. *Creativity and Taoism: A Study of Chinese Philosophy, Art and Poetry*. New York: Harper & Row, 1963.

———. *Tao: A New Way of Thinking—A Translation of the Tao Tê Ching with an Introduction and Commentaries*. New York: Harper & Row, 1975.

Chang, Garma C. C. *The Practice of Zen*. New York: Harper & Row, 1959.

Chuang Tzu. *The Complete Works of Chuang Tzu*. Translated by Burton Watson. New York: Columbia University Press, 1968.

Deshimaru, Taisen. *Shōbōgenzō: Le Trésor de la Vraie Loi*. Paris: Le Courrier du Livre, 1970.

Dewey, John. *The Quest for Certainty*. New York: Putnam, 1929.

Dōgen Kigen. *Dōgen zenji zenshū* [Complete works of Zen Master Dōgen]. Edited by Ōkubo Dōshū. 2 vols. Tokyo: Chikuma Shobō, 1969–1970.

Doi, L. Takeo. "Morita Therapy and Psychoanalysis." *Psychologia* 5 (1962):117–123.

_____. "Amae: A Key Concept for Understanding Japanese Personality Structure." In *Japanese Culture and Behavior*, edited by Takie Sugiyama Lebra and William P. Lebra. Honolulu: The University Press of Hawaii, 1974.

Dumoulin, Heinrich. "Das Buch Genjōkōan aus dem *Shōbōgenzō* des Zen Meisters Dōgen." *Monumenta Nipponica* 15(3-4)(1959-1960): 217-232.

_____. *A History of Zen Buddhism*. Translated by Paul Peachey. Boston: Beacon Press, 1963.

Freud, Sigmund. *The Standard Edition of the Complete Psychological Works of Sigmund Freud*. Edited and translated by James Strachey. 24 vols. London: The Hogarth Press and the Institute of Psycho-Analysis, 1953-.

Fromm, Erich, Suzuki, D. T., and DeMartino, Richard. *Zen Buddhism and Psychoanalysis*. New York: Harper & Row, 1960.

Fung, Yu-lan. *A History of Chinese Philosophy*. Translated by Derk Bodde. 2 vols. Princeton: Princeton University Press, 1952.

Heidegger, Martin. *Discourse on Thinking*. Translated by John M. Anderson and E. Hans Freund. New York: Harper & Row, 1966.

_____. *Poetry, Language, Thought*. Translated by Albert Hofstadter. New York: Harper & Row, 1971.

Henderson, Harold G. *An Introduction to Haiku: An Anthology of Poems and Poets from Bashō to Shiki*. Garden City, New York: Doubleday Anchor Books, 1958.

Inada, Kenneth K. *Nāgārjuna: A Translation of His Mūlamadhyamaka-kārikā with an Introductory Essay*. Tokyo: The Hokuseido Press, 1970.

James, William. "A World of Pure Experience." In *Essays in Radical Empiricism and a Pluralistic Universe*. New York: E. P. Dutton, 1971.

Jung, Carl G. *The Collected Works of Carl G. Jung*. Translated by R. F. C. Hull. 18 vols. Princeton: Princeton University Press (for The Bollingen Foundation), 1971.

Kaketa, Katsumi. "Psychoanalysis in Japan." *Psychologia* 1(1958): 247-252.

Kaltenmark, Max. *Lao Tzu and Taoism*. Translated by Roger Greaves. Stanford: Stanford University Press, 1969.

Kalupahana, David J. *Buddhist Philosophy: A Historical Analysis*. Honolulu: The University Press of Hawaii, 1976.

_____. "Translation of Nāgārjuna's *Mūlamadhyamakakārikā*." Unpublished manuscript. Honolulu, 1978.

Kapleau, Philip, ed. and trans. *The Three Pillars of Zen: Teaching, Practice and Enlightenment*. New York: Harper & Row, 1966.

Kasulis, T. P. "Zen Buddhism, Freud, and Jung." *The Eastern Buddhist*, NS 10, 1(May 1977):68-91.

Kim, Hee-jin. *Dōgen Kigen—Mystical Realist.* Tucson: University of Arizona Press, 1975.

Kora, Takehisa. "Morita Therapy." In *Memorial Lectures for Professor Kora.* Tokyo: Jikei University, 1964.

Kora, Takehisa, and Sato, Koji. "Morita Therapy—A Psychotherapy in the Way of Zen." *Psychologia* 1(1958):219-225.

Lao Tsu. *Tao Te Ching.* Translated by Gia-Fu Feng and Jane English. New York: Vintage Books, 1972.

Masuda, Koh, ed. *Kenkyusha's New Japanese-English Dictionary.* Tokyo: Kenkyusha Ltd., 1974.

Masunaga Reihō. *Eihei Shōbōgenzō: Dōgen no shūkyō* [*Eihei Shōbōgenzō:* Dōgen's religion]. Tokyo: Shunjūsha, 1956.

Matsunaga, Daigan, and Matsunaga, Alicia. *Foundation of Japanese Buddhism.* 2 vols. Los Angeles: Buddhist Books International, 1974.

Miura, Isshū, and Sasaki, Ruth Fuller. *Zen Dust.* New York: Harcourt. Brace & World, 1966.

Murti, T. R. V. *The Central Philosophy of Buddhism: A Study of the Mādhyamika System.* London: Allen and Unwin, 1960.

Nakamura, Hajime. *Ways of Thinking of Eastern Peoples: India-China-Tibet-Japan.* Honolulu: East-West Center Press, 1964.

Naranjo, Claudio, and Ornstein, Robert E. *On the Psychology of Meditation.* New York: Viking Press, 1971.

Nishida, Kitarō. *A Study of Good.* Translated by Valdo H. Viglielmo. Tokyo: Japanese Government Printing Bureau, 1960.

————. *Zen no kenkyū* [Study of good]. In vol. 47 of *Nihon no meicho* [Famous works of Japan]. Tokyo: Chūōkōronsha, 1977.

Nishitani, Keiji. "What Is Religion?" Translated by Janice Rowe. *Philosophical Studies of Japan* 2(1960):21-64.

Reps, Paul, comp. *Zen Flesh, Zen Bones: A Collection of Zen and Pre-Zen Writings.* New York: Doubleday, n.d.

Reynolds, David K. *Morita Psychotherapy.* Berkeley: University of California Press, 1976.

Ricoeur, Paul. *Husserl: An Analysis of His Phenomenology.* Evanston, Illinois: Northwestern University Press, 1967.

Rosemont, Henry, Jr. "The Meaning Is the Use: *Kōan* and *Mondō* as Linguistic Tools of the Zen Masters." *Philosophy East and West* 20(April 1970):109-119.

Sartre, Jean-Paul. *The Transcendence of the Ego: An Existentialist Theory of Consciousness.* Translated by Forrest Williams and Robert Kirkpatrick. New York: Farrar, Straus and Giroux, 1957.

Sasaki, Joshu Roshi. *Buddha Is the Center of Gravity.* Translated by Fusako Akinu. San Cristobal, New Mexico: Lama Foundation, 1974.

Sato, Koji. "Psychotherapeutic Implications of Zen." *Psychologia* 1(1958): 213-218.

Shibayama, Zenkei. *A Flower Does Not Talk: Zen Essays.* Translated by Sumiko Kudo. Tokyo: Charles E. Tuttle, 1970.

_____. *Zen Comments on the Mumonkan.* New York: Harper & Row, 1974.

Streng, Frederick J. *Emptiness: A Study in Religious Meaning.* New York: Abingdon Press, 1967.

Suzuki, D. T. *Rinzai no kihonshisō: Rinzai roku ni okeru "jin" shisō no kenkyū* [The fundamental ideas of Rinzai: a study of the idea of "man" in the *Rinzai Records*]. Tokyo: Chūōkōronsha, 1949.

_____. *An Introduction to Zen Buddhism.* New York: Grove Press, 1964.

_____. *The Zen Doctrine of No-Mind: The Significance of the Sutra of Hui-Neng (Wei-Lang).* London: Rider and Co., 1959.

Takahashi Masanobu. *Shōbōgenzō: Gendaiyaku* [*Shōbōgenzō:* a modern Japanese translation]. Tokyo: Risōsha, 1971–1972.

Terada Tōru and Mizuno Yaoko. *Dōgen.* Vols. 12 and 13 of the series *Nihonshisō taikei* [Outlines of Japanese thought]. Tokyo: Iwanami Shoten, 1970–1972.

Uchiyama, Kosho Roshi. *Approach to Zen: The Reality of Zazen/Modern Civilization and Zen.* San Francisco: Japan Publications, 1973.

Waddell, Norman, and Abe, Masao, trans. "Dōgen's Bendōwa." *The Eastern Buddhist,* NS 4, 1(1971):124–157.

_____. "Shōbōgenzō Genjōkōan." *The Eastern Buddhist,* NS 5, 2(1972):129–140.

_____. "Dōgen's Fukanzazengi and Shōbōgenzō Zazengi." *The Eastern Buddhist,* NS 6, 2(1973):115–128.

Waley, Arthur. *The Way and Its Power: A Study of the Tao Tê Ching and Its Place in Chinese Thought.* New York: Grove Press, 1958.

Watsuji Tetsurō. *Watsuji Tetsurō zenshū* [Complete works of Watsuji Tetsurō]. Tokyo: Iwanami Shoten, 1962. Reprinted 1977.

_____. "The Significance of Ethics as the Study of Man." Translated by David Dilworth. *Monumenta Nipponica* 26(3–4)(1971):395–413.

Welch, Holmes. *Taoism: The Parting of the Way.* Boston: Beacon Press, 1965.

Yampolsky, Philip B., trans. *The Platform Sutra of the Sixth Patriarch.* New York: Columbia University Press, 1967.

_____. *The Zen Master Hakuin: Selected Writings.* New York: Columbia University Press, 1971.

# Glossary

Chinese names and terms are followed by the notation (Ch). All others are Japanese.

AKIYAMA Hanji 秋山範二
amaeru 甘える

Baō 馬翁
basho 場所
Bashō 芭蕉
"Bendōwa" 辨道話
bugyō 奉行
Butchō 佛頂
butsudō 佛道

ch'an (Ch) 禪
ch'ang tao (Ch) 常道
Chao-chou (Ch) 趙州
CH'ÊNG Hao (Ch) 程顥
Chuang Tzǔ (Ch) 莊子

daigi 大疑
daikangi 大歡喜
daishi 大死
datsuraku 脱落
dōchu no kufū 動中の工夫
DŌGEN Kigen 道元希玄
dokusan 獨參
DŌKYŌ Etan 道鏡慧端
Dōrin 道林
dōtoku 道得

Enō 慧能
enryo 遠慮

fa (Ch) 法
Fa-yen (Ch) 法眼
Fukanzazengi 普勸坐禪儀
fushiryō 不思量

Gantō 巖頭
genjōkōan (su) 現成公案(す)
genjō su 現成す
Gensha 玄沙
gidan 疑團

HAKU Kyoi 白居易
HAKUIN Ekaku 白隱慧鶴
hishiryō 非思量
hō 法
Hōgen 法眼
honbunnin 本分人
hongaku 本覚
Hsüan-sha (Ch) 玄沙
Hui-nêng (Ch) 慧能

immo 恁麽
issai shujō shitsu u busshō 一切衆生悉
　有佛性

jên (Ch) 仁
jiko 自己
jijōgoi 自淨其意
jisetsu 時節
Jōshū 趙州
Ju-ching (Ch) 如淨
junsui keiken 純粋経験

kaku 覚
kambun 漢文
kango no kotoba 漢語の言葉
keireki 經歴
Kennin-ji 建仁寺
Kisei 歸省
kōan 公案
kōangenjō 公案現成
kojin 個人
kū 空
Kuei-shêng (Ch) 歸省
kūmu 空無
kun 訓
k'ung (Ch) 空
kyōryaku 經歴

Lao Tzŭ (Ch) 老子
Lin-chi (Ch) 臨濟

makusa 莫作
mikkyō 密教
ming (Ch) 命
MIZUNO Yaoko 水野弥穂子
mo-chao-ch'an (Ch) 默照禪
mokushō zen 默照禪
mondō 問答
MORITA Shōma 森田正馬
mu 無
muga 無我
mui shinnin 無位眞人
mujū 無住

munen 無念
mushin 無心
musō 無相
Myōzen 明全

naikan 內觀
Nan-ch'üan (Ch) 南泉
Nansen 南泉
NAN-YANG Hui-chung (Ch) 南陽慧忠
NAN'YŌ Echū 南陽慧忠
nikon 而今
ningen 人間
NISHIDA Kitarō 西田幾多郎
Nyojō 如淨

on 音

p'o (Ch) 樸
Po Chü-i (Ch) 白居易

Rinzai 臨濟
Ryūshaku-ji 立石寺

SA 作
sanzen 參禪
satori 悟
SEKISŌ Soen 石霜楚圓
sesshin 攝心
SHIDŌ Bunan 至道無難
SHIH-SHUANG Ch'u-yüan (Ch) 石霜楚圓
shikaku 始覚
shikantaza 祇管打坐
shinjin 身心
shinjindatsuraku 身心脫落
shinjin'ichinyo 身心一如
shinkeishitsu 神経質
shiryō 思量
shiza 死坐
shō 證

shoakumakusa 諸悪莫作
shōbō 正法
*Shōbōgenzō* 正法眼藏
Shōin-ji 松蔭寺
SHŌJU Rōjin 正受老人
Shōtoku 聖徳
Shou-shan (Ch) 首山
shu 修
shugyō 修行
shushō 修證
Shuzan 首山
shuzenbugyō 衆善奉行
Sōtō shū 曹洞宗

TAKAHASHI Masanobu 高橋賢陳
TANABE Hajime 田辺元
tao (Ch) 道
Tao-lin (Ch) 道林
*Tao Tê Ching* (Ch) 道徳經
tê (Ch) 德
TERADA Tōru 寺田透

u 有
uji 有時

wago no kotoba 和語の言葉
waka 和歌
WATSUJI Tetsurō 和辻哲郎
wu (Ch) 無
wu-chu (Ch) 無住
wu-hsiang (Ch) 無相
wu-nien (Ch) 無念
wu-wei (Ch) 無爲

YAKUSAN Gudō 薬山弘道
Yen-t'ou (Ch) 巖頭
yōshin 用心
yu (Ch) 有
YÜEH-SHAN Hung-tao (Ch) 薬山弘道
yu-hsin (Ch) 有心
yu-hsin-hsin (Ch) 有心心
yung-hsin (Ch) 用心
yu-wu (Ch) 有無

zazen 坐禪
"Zazengi" 坐禪儀
"Zazenshin" 坐禪箴
zen 禪
zesshobukkyō 是諸佛教

# Index

son, 51, 122; two monks and maiden, 46, 57; Yakusan's without-thinking, 71–72. *See also* Koan
Striking, 121
Subject-object, 57, 90, 91. *See also* Noesis-noema
Suchness. *See Immo*
Suffering, 55–56, 150n. *See also* Attachment
Śūnyatā. *See* Emptiness

Tao, 29–32. *See also* Nonbeing; Taoism
Taoism, 29–38; absolute and relative in, 29–36; cosmogony of, 29–36; and creativity, 36–38; and Zen, 36–37. *See also* Nonbeing; *Wu-wei*
Tao-lin. *See* Dōrin
*Tao Tê Ching*, 29–31, 36–37, 42
Thought: as intermediary stage, 60, 62–64; Nishida on, 62–64; and no-thought, 43–45; in zazen, 44–45. *See also* Analysis; Distinctions; No-mind; Reflection; Without-thinking
Time, 19, 78–83
True person of no status, 51–52, 93, 122, 132, 154. *See also* Person
Truth, 22, 93, 119–120, 153

UCHIYAMA Kōshō, Master: on zazen, 44–45
*Uji*, 78–83
Uncarved block *(p'o)*, 37

WATSUJI Tetsurō, 155n. 1
*Weltanschauung*, 101–102
Western culture, and Zen, 123–124, 145–146, 150–154
Wisdom *(prajñā)*, 25, 61, 97, 114
Without-thinking: as compassion, 97–99; in context of nothingness, 128, 130–133; and emptiness, 72; and

Great Doubt, 112–116; and language, 133–139; and Nonbeing, 160n. 18; as relationship, 128, 130–133; and thinking/not-thinking, 71–77, 100, 114; and Zen action, 139–141; and Zen training, 118–122. *See also* Prereflective experience
WU-MÊN Hui-k'ai. *See* MUMON Ekai
*Wu-wei* (nondoing), 36–38, 95, 138

YAKUSAN Gudō (Ch: YÜEH-SHAN Hung-tao), 71–72
YASUTANI Hakuun, Master: on *mu* koan, 12
Yen-t'ou. *See* Gantō
YÜEH-SHAN Hung-tao. *See* YAKUSAN Gudō

Zazen: definition of, 70; Dōgen on, 70–86; in midst of activity *(dōchū no kufū)*, 111–112, 123; physiology of, 162–163n; thinking in, 44–45; in the West, 146, 153–154. *See also* Cultivation-authentication; Without-thinking
Zen: action in, 95–97, 128, 130–141; and Christianity, 146; ethics in, 93–99, 141; as a humanism, 151–154; in Japanese culture, 3, 9, 40–41, 124, 128–133, 145–146, 148–150; and Morita therapy, 149–150; origin of term for, 66; and philosophy, ix–xi; as religion, x–xi, 55, 154; Rinzai and Sōtō orders of, 104–105; training in, 59–60, 104–105, 116–122 *(see also* Monastery, Zen); in the West, 145–146, 150–154. *See also* Person
Zen interview *(sanzen)*, 41–42, 119–120, 134–135, 137
Zen sickness, 111–112

## ☒ Production Notes

This book was designed by Roger Eggers and
typeset on the Unified Composing System by
The University Press of Hawaii.

The text typeface is Compugraphic Caledonia
and the display typeface is Compugraphic Palatino.

Offset presswork and binding were done by Halliday
Lithograph. Text paper is Glatfelter P & S Offset,
basis 55.